BUSINESS LETTER WRITING

Sheryl Lindsell-Roberts

MACMILLAN • USA

Macmillan General Reference
A Simon & Schuster Macmillan Company
1633 Broadway
New York, NY 10019-6785

An Arco Book

MACMILLAN is a registered trademark of Macmillan, Inc.
ARCO is a registered trademark of Prentice-Hall, Inc.

Library of Congress Cataloging-in-Publication Data

Lindsell-Roberts, Sheryl.
Business letter writing / Sheryl Lindsell-Roberts
    p.   cm
"An Arco book"—T.p. verso
Includes index.
ISBN: 0-02-860014-2
1. Business writing. I. Title.
HF5718.3.L56   1994   94-18524
808'.066651—dc20   CIP

Manufactured in the United States of America

10   9   8   7   6   5   4

CONTENTS

PART III • REFERENCE SECTION

Dear Colleague,

Business people at all levels—from the neophyte professional to the articulate CEO—experience moments of self-doubt when it comes to writing a letter. Perhaps you've said:

- I keep putting off writing this letter because I don't know where to start.
- This letter sounds so dull.
- How can I say *no* tactfully?
- I hate to send dunning letters to my customers. I'm afraid of losing their business.
- I saw this wonderful job advertised. How can I write a dynamite application letter?

So, when you feel that brief moment of panic, relax! You're in good company.

Business letters account for about 90 percent of all written correspondence—a powerful tool by any standards. A well-written letter can mean advancement for your career, profit for your company, and satisfaction for your clients or customers. In this high-tech world of spelling, grammar, and style checkers; clip art; mail merge; and automated formatting, the computer can supply the mechanics of a letter. But in order for your letter to stand out from the myriad of others that compete for the reader's attention each day, you must unite the mechanics with the human factor—the reader. Don't let your dynamic ideas be overshadowed by mediocre writing.

This comprehensive book has been carefully written to sharpen that vital business tool to help you become a skilled letter writer who gets results, prompts action, influences decisions, stimulates business, and maintains good will. This book will become your valued desktop companion. In addition to letters for nearly every business situation, it contains guidelines for grammar and punctuation, lists of commonly misspelled and misused words, and proper forms of address.

Feel free to use the examples in this book verbatim or mix and match them to befit your own situations. Instantly, you'll be creating letters with competence and confidence.

Best wishes,

SLR

A special thanks to all the business people who allowed me to pepper this book with their attention-getting letters.

To my dearest mom . . .

known to the rest of the world as Ethel Lorenz I
owe my letter writing talents to you. All the years I was
growing up, I remember family and friends coming to you
with their problems. You would always write a letter on
their behalf; and shortly thereafter, each one would report
having received an apology, a free sample, or some
satisfactory course of action. A friend once said, "When
Ethel writes a letter, the paper burns."

Thanks, mom, for that and so much more.

Sheryl

PART · I

GENERAL INFORMATION

CHAPTER ONE

PARTS, PLACEMENT, AND STYLES

Are you often puzzled by the number of parts in a letter and where each part goes? If so, this chapter will take all the mystery out of letter parts.

LETTER PARTS

This section will identify all the parts that can be included in a letter. Some are used in all letters; others depend on the circumstances. At the end of this section, you will see a letter in which all the parts appear.

(1) Date Line

The current date should be written with arabic numerals and no abbreviations.

> September 16, 19—
> 16 September, 19— (military or European usage)

(2) Mailing or In-House Notations

Mailing notations (special delivery, certified mail, registered mail, air mail, by messenger) or in-house notations (personal, confidential) are placed two lines below the date—in all capital letters.

> PERSONAL
> CERTIFIED MAIL

(3) Inside Address

The inside address should start four lines below the date line. (If a mailing or in-house notation is used, the inside address should start two lines below the notation.) The inside address includes any or all of the following: the name of the person to whom you are writing; the person's title; company name; street address; and city, state, and ZIP code.

> Mr. Thom Collins, President
> Liquorland, U.S.A.
> 164 Bay Road
> Oklahoma City, OK 73125-5050

NOTES:

a. Whether the person's title appears on the same line as the name or on the following line will be determined by the length. Try to square the address as much as possible. If the title appears on the same line, place a comma between the name and title. If it appears on the next line, dispense with the comma.

> Mr. Thom Collins, President
> - *or* -
> Mr. Thom Collins
> President

b. Mail is delivered to the address element on the line above the city, state, and ZIP. Therefore, if you want the letter delivered to a post office box, place the post office box number underneath (or instead of) the street address.

> 607 Arboretum Boulevard
> P.O. Box 7344
> Austin, TX 78959-7344

c. Post office guidelines require that you use the nine-digit ZIP code, which is broken out as follows:

01970-6811

   ⌊1⌋   1. (One of ten national areas [0–9])
   ⌊ 2 ⌋   2. (Sectional center facility of major P.O.)
    ⌊ 3 ⌋   3. (Associate P.O. in sectional center facility)
     ⌊ 4 ⌋   4. (Block or Building)

d. Post office guidelines also require that you use the two-letter state abbreviations for the inside address.

Two-Letter State Abbreviations

Alabama	AL	Missouri	MO
Alaska	AK	Montana	MT
Arizona	AZ	Nebraska	NE
Arkansas	AR	Nevada	NV
California	CA	New Hampshire	NH
Canal Zone	CZ	New Jersey	NJ
Colorado	CO	New Mexico	NM
Connecticut	CT	New York	NY
Delaware	DE	North Carolina	NC
District of		North Dakota	ND
Columbia	DC	Ohio	OH
Florida	FL	Oklahoma	OK
Georgia	GA	Oregon	OR
Guam	GU	Pennsylvania	PA
Hawaii	HI	Puerto Rico	PR
Idaho	ID	Rhode Island	
Illinois	IL	South Carolina	SC
Indiana	IN	South Dakota	SD
Iowa	IA	Tennessee	TN
Kansas	KS	Texas	TX
Kentucky	KY	Utah	UT
Louisiana	LA	Vermont	VT
Maine	ME	Virginia	VA
Maryland	MD	Virgin Islands	VI
Massachusetts	MA	Washington	WA
Michigan	MI	West Virginia	WV
Minnesota	MN	Wisconsin	WI
Mississippi	MS	Wyoming	WY

(4) Attention Line

The attention line is used when you write directly to a company and want the letter directed to a particular person and/or department. It also indicates that the letter should be handled by someone else if the addressee is not available. You can use any of the following styles:

ATTENTION ELSIE HERSCH

Attention Personnel Manager

Attention: Accounting Department

P & M Construction Company
34 Madison Avenue
Columbus, OH 43004
  (double space)
Attention: Paul Sharfin

P & M Construction Company
ATTENTION PAUL SHARFIN
34 Madison Avenue
Columbus, OH 43004

(5) Salutation

The salutation is placed two lines below the address. It should correspond directly to the first line of the inside address.

Inside Address	Closed Punctuation	Open Punctuation
Mr. John Smith	Dear Mr. Smith: Dear John: (informal)	Dear Mr. Smith Dear John (informal)
Ms. Joan Smith	Dear Ms. Smith: Dear Joan: (informal)	Dear Ms. Smith Dear Joan (informal)
Mr. and Mrs. John Smith	Dear Mr. and Mrs. Smith: Dear John and Joan: (informal)	Dear Mr. and Mrs. Smith Dear John and Joan (informal)
Messrs. Max and Harry Lorenz	Dear Messrs. Lorenz: Dear Max and Harry: (informal)	Dear Messrs. Lorenz Dear Max and Harry (informal)
Mmes. Ethel and Marilyn Lorenz	Dear Mmes. Lorenz: Dear Ethel and Marilyn: (informal)	Dear Mmes. Lorenz Dear Ethel and Marilyn (informal)
Messrs. James Taylor and Bob Grant	Dear Messrs. Taylor and Grant: Dear James and Bob: (informal)	Dear Messrs. Taylor and Grant Dear James and Bob (informal)
Mmes. Sally Jones and Jan Fox	Dear Mmes. Jones and Fox: Dear Sally and Jan: (informal)	Dear Mmes. Jones and Fox Dear Sally and Jan (informal)
The Comptroller	Dear Sir or Madam:	Dear Sir or Madam
A & D Corporation	Ladies and Gentlemen:	Ladies and Gentlemen
Unknown person or company	To Whom This May Concern:	To Whom This May Concern

(6) Subject Line

The subject line is considered part of the letter, not the heading; therefore, it should always be placed two lines below the salutation. The purpose of the subject line is to direct the reader to the theme of the letter. You can use any of the following styles:

SUBJECT: ACCOUNT NO. 2261-B
Re: Special Rebate
Subject: Policy No. 453534 454
In re: Invoice No. CO-3434

(7) Body (Message)

The body of the letter is generally single spaced with double spacing between paragraphs.

a. The opening paragraph is relatively short and introduces the letter.

Thank you for your letter of July 16 calling our attention to our mistake in filling your order.

Our research staff has successfully solved the problem of insulating older homes about which you inquired in your letter of May 10.

b. The middle paragraph(s) supports the opening and/or provides additional information.

In its annual report, the X Y Z Fire Insurance Company stated that our community has suffered the least fire damage of any district in the state. Of course this means that your belongings are safer than those of your distant neighbors. But more important is the fact that your family is well protected from the dangers of ravaging fire.

c. The final paragraph is short and serves as a summation, request, suggestion, or look to the future.

The enclosed brochure should answer your questions. If you need more information, please let us know.

If you would like to take advantage of this order, please sign the enclosed form and return it to me in the enclosed envelope.

(8) Complimentary Closing

The complimentary closing will appear two lines below the last line of the body. Only the first word is capitalized.

formal: Yours truly, Very truly yours, Yours very truly, Respectfully, Respectfully yours,

informal: Sincerely, Sincerely yours, Cordially, Cordially yours,

personal: Best wishes, As always, Regards, Kindest regards,

(9) Signature Line

Personal signatures can be handled in any of the following ways:

Very truly yours,
Jon Allan
Jon Allan

Very truly yours,
Jon Allan
Jon Allan, Process Manager

Very truly yours,
ALLEGRO, INC.
Jon Allan
Jon Allan, Process Manager

Very truly yours,
Jon Allan
Jon Allan
Process Manager

(10) Reference Initials

Reference initials are used to identify the author of the letter and/or the typist. They should appear at the left margin, two lines below the signature line. If you are writing your own letter, there is no need for initials. You can use any of the following styles:

HLorenz/lz
HL:lz

HL/LZ
lz

(11) Enclosure Notation

The enclosure notation appears on the line directly below the reference initials when anything is being sent along with the letter. In some offices, when something is attached rather than enclosed, the word *Attachment* will appear in place of *Enclosure*. You can use any of the following styles:

Enclosure
Enc.
Encls.
1 Attachment

1 Enc.
Attachments: 2
Enc. (2)
Enclosure:
      1. Purchase Order No. 3434
      2. Check No. 567

(12) Copy Notation

When a copy of the letter is being sent to a third person, a notation to that effect is made directly below the enclosure notation or reference initials. The *cc* notation is a holdover from the days of carbon copies. Many offices are now using *pc* (for photo copy) instead.

If the author doesn't want the addressee to know that a copy is being forwarded to a third party, use *bc* for blind copy. This notation appears on the office copy and third-party copy only. No notation is made on the original. You can use any of the above styles.

PC: Arlene Karp	bc: Arlene Karp
CC: Arlene Karp	Copy to: Arlene Karp

(13) Postscript

A postscript should be used sparingly because it can appear as an afterthought, indicating a lack of organization. Sometimes, however, it is used for emphasis. It should appear two lines below your last notation, and the *P.S.* notation is no longer used.

jt
Enclosure

I'll call you for lunch next Friday!

LETTER PLACEMENT

Your letter should be vertically and horizontally centered so that the margins form an imaginary frame around the words. The following guidelines will assist you in determining the placement of your letter.

Length	Word Count	On Computer	On Typewriter
short	125 or less	1.25" left and right 1.25" top and bottom	19–20 lines from top 17–67 margins (pica) 25–75 margins (elite)
medium	126–225	1" left and right 1" top and bottom	15–18 lines from top 17–67 margins (pica) 20–80 margins (elite)
long (one page)	226 or more	.75" left and right .75" top and bottom	10–12 lines from top 12–72 margins (pica) 15–85 margins (elite)

Lighting **&** **D**ecorating, Inc.
143 East Railway Avenue, Paterson, NJ 07503
(201) 345-1234

- **SEARCHLIGHTS**

- **SOUND**

- **BALL FIELD LIGHTING**

- **DISPLAY LIGHTING**

- **FLOOD LIGHTING**

- **FURNITURE RENTAL**

- **N.J. STATE LICENSE #3110**

April 12, 19— ———————————————————— (1) Date Line

CERTIFIED MAIL ———————————————— (2) Mailing Notation

Marric Enterprises ————————————— (3) Inside Address
Attention Thomas James ————————— (4) Attention Line
24 Blazer Way
Spring Valley, NY 10977

Gentlemen: ——————————————————— (5) Salutation

Subject: Hunting and Fishing Contract ———— (6) Subject Line

I am enclosing the contract we agreed upon stipulat-
ing all the terms and conditions of the hunting and
fishing show that will take place at the Besen
Community College Field House during the week of   (7) Body
May 1.   or Message

Can we meet for lunch on either Monday, Tuesday, or
Wednesday of next week to finalize the details? If
none of these dates is convenient, please call my
office so that we can arrange a mutually convenient
time.

Sincerely yours, ——————————————— (8) Complimentary Closing

LIGHTING & DECORATING, INC.

Noel Christie, President ————————————— (9) Signature Line

sll ———————————————————————— (10) Reference Line
Enclosure ————————————————————— (11) Enclosure Notation
cc: Besen Community College ——————————— (12) Copy Notation

The ski show contract will be ready next week.—— (13) Postscript

LETTER STYLES

Choosing a letter style is a big step in creating the proper impression. The style may be dictated by your company or may be your choice. If the decision is yours, be guided by the following:

- *Pay close attention to the letterhead.* Some companies have letterheads that will complement one style over another.

- *Know the image your company is trying to project.* A traditional letter style (block or semiblock) will project the image of a solid, well-established company. An informal style (simplified) may work well for younger people but may appear unconventional to older people.

These are the four popular letter styles. An example of each follows.

Letter Style	*Characteristics and Comments*
Full block	• Everything starts at the left margin; there is no need to set any tabs. • Efficient, businesslike, and very popular. • Critics feel it looks somewhat crowded.
Block or Modified Block	• The date and complimentary closing are slightly to the right of center. • Everything else starts at the left margin. • Involves setting one tab. • Very traditional and very popular.
Semiblock	• Identical to Block (above), except the first line of each paragraph is indented.
Simplified	• Involves setting two tabs. • Salutation and complimentary closing are omitted, everything else is in full block. • Recommended by the Administrative Management Society as the most efficient of all styles. • Critics say it lacks warmth and is too unconventional.

Full Block Style

Current date

Addressee
Street Address
City, State ZIP

Salutation:

Re: Full Block Style

This easy-to-keyboard letter is becoming more
and more popular and is widely used in many
of today's modern offices.

It is a very efficient style because everything
begins at the left margin, thereby eliminating
the need for tabs.

We are now in an era where productivity is a
major concern, and this style will increase the
flow of paperwork.

Very truly yours,

Name

xx

Modified Block Style

Current date

Addressee
Street Address
City, State ZIP

Salutation:

Re: Modified Block Style

Modified block has traditionally been the most
commonly used of all letter styles.

The most notable difference between this style
and the full block is that the date and complimentary closing start at the center, or slightly
to the right of center. Note that the subject
line, the inside address, and all paragraphs
remain flush with the left margin.

This letter style is appealing to the eye and is
very popular.

Very truly yours,

Name

xx

Semiblock Style

Current date

Addressee
Street Address
City, State ZIP

Salutation:

   Re: Semiblock Style

   The distinguishing features of this letter style
are that the subject line is indented and all
paragraphs are indented five to seven spaces
from the left margin.

   It is important to remember that two tabs
must be set: one for the date and complimentary closing and one for the indentation of the
subject line and paragraphs.

   If you are employed in an office where
maximum productivity is not essential, this style
may be preferred.

Very truly yours,

Name

xx

Simplified Style

Current date

Addressee
Street Address
City, State ZIP

SIMPLIFIED STYLE

No longer do you have to worry about selecting
the appropriate salutation and complimentary
closing. This streamlined letter style has completely eliminated them.

The subject line—with no notation—appears
in all capital letters three lines below the inside
address, and the body of the letter appears
three lines below the subject line. The writer's
name appears four lines below the body; also in
capital letters. Note that everything is flush
with the left margin.

This letter style is not commonly used, but it is
expected to be a style of the future.

NAME

xx

Two-Page Letters

When typing a two-page letter, use letterhead for the first page and matching plain paper for the rest of the pages. When you divide a paragraph between pages, at least two lines must remain on the first page and at least two lines should be carried to the second page. Never divide a three-line paragraph and never carry a complimentary closing over to a second page without having at least two lines above it.

The heading on the second page should appear as follows:

MODIFIED OR SEMIBLOCK

Ms. Katherine Wertalik   Page 2   October 2, 19—

FULL BLOCK OR SIMPLIFIED

Ms. Katherine Wertalik
Page 2
October 2, 19—

FOLDING THE LETTER

1. Standard (8½ by 11 inch) stationery being placed in a No. 10 (9½ by 4⅛ inch) envelope, Monarch (7¼ by 10½ inch) stationery being placed in a No. 7 (7½ by 3⅞ inch) envelope, or Baronial (5½ by 8½ inch) stationery being placed in a No. 6¾ (6½ by 3⅝ inch) envelope is folded as follows:

    a. Fold the bottom of the letter approximately one-third up and make a crease.

    b. Fold the top one-third down and make a crease.

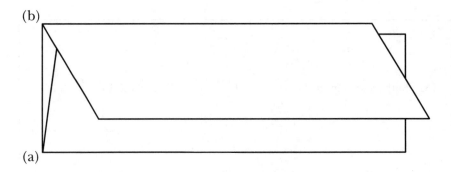

2. Standard stationery being placed in a No. 6¾ (6½ by 3⅝ inch) envelope is folded as follows:

    a. Fold in half, long side up.

    b. Fold in thirds across.

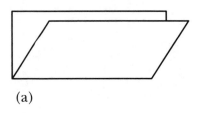

(a)

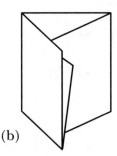

(b)

3. Stationery being placed in a window envelope will be folded as follows:

    a. Fold the bottom of the letter approximately one-third up and make a crease.

    b. Fold the top one-third back and make a crease. The inside address should be on the outside and placed in the envelope so that it is visible through the window.

(a)

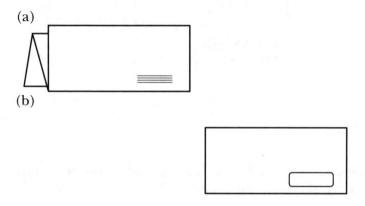

(b)

ENVELOPES

Envelopes should match the stationery in color and style. Use the following postal guidelines to address an envelope.

1. The address should be single spaced in the block style. The address should appear on the envelope as it appears on the inside address.

2. All in-house notations should be typed two to three lines below the return address and should align with the left margin.

3. All postal notations should be typed under the area where the stamp will be placed.

The name and address should be typed in all capital letters, with no punctuation. (Use RD for Road, AVE for Avenue, ST for Street, etc.)

RETURN ADDRESS

PERSONAL

SPECIAL DELIVERY

JANICE TEISCH
JANICE TEISCH & ASSOCIATES
7 INLAND RD
NEW CITY   NY   10956

- If the addressee uses both a street address and a post office box, the line directly above the city, state, and ZIP code is where the letter will be delivered.

- If a room or suite number is used, it should immediately follow the street address on the same line.

  56 FIFTH AVE ROOM 304

INTEROFFICE MEMOS

The main purpose of the interoffice memo is to transmit ideas, decisions, and suggestions to another member or members of your organization. If an organization uses memos frequently, it will generally have the forms printed. The forms can be half sheets or full sheets, depending on the length of the message.

On a memo you:

Omit	**Retain**
inside address	body or message
salutation	reference initials
complimentary closing	enclosure notation
signature	copy notation

1. Start the body of the memo three spaces below the heading.

2. Align the left margin with the typewritten portion of the heading, and set the right margin so that it is equal to the left.

3. Single space the paragraphs in block style, double spacing between each paragraph.

4. When typing a memo on a blank sheet of paper, start $1^{1}/_{2}$ inches from the top. Any of the following headings may be used:

To:	TO:
From:	FROM:
Date:	DATE:
Subject:	SUBJECT:

Date:	Date:
To:	TO:
From:	FROM:
Subject:	SUBJECT:

CHAPTER • TWO

HALLMARKS OF AN EFFECTIVE LETTER

Writing involves a craft you have to learn and a talent you must possess. Neither is common and both are essential.

—Goethe

ORGANIZATION, TONE, AND WORD SELECTION

Once you have established the "look" of your letter, the next hurdles are organization, tone, and word selection.

Organization

What will you say? How will you say it? Write a brief outline, jotting down the key points. Do not include everything you want to say—just the highlights. To save time, use a computer or abbreviated long-hand. (If you are responding to someone else's letter, use the margins to make notes.)

1. Identify the main purpose of your letter.

2. Identify all the secondary purposes.

3. List all the points that need to be covered. In your outline, jot down every detail you think of. This is known as *brainstorming*.

4. Review the list and eliminate any items that can be omitted without sacrificing completeness or understandability.

5. Check your plan for sequencing.

For example, let us assume you are placing an order for 1 box of 3-ring binders. You must include:

Size: 8½ by 11 inches—2" spine

Item No.: AB-456-2

Method of Payment: (Account No., C.O.D., check, etc.)

Shipment: UPS

Need by: October 5 (Never use As Soon As Possible. ASAP isn't a date.)

Once you have outlined the necessary information, go back and number each of the items in the order in which they should appear in the letter.

Tone

Always put yourself in the shoes of the reader, and ask yourself these questions. If I were the reader. . .

- Would I be glad to receive this letter?

- How would I react/respond?

- Would I be glad to hear the news?

Once you have answered these questions, you will begin to "experience" the reader's reaction. Use a natural and relaxed writing style and a positive tone. How you deliver the message will influence your reader as much as the message itself. Look at the messages that follow.

| Courteous | Yes: | Thank you for your time and effort in applying for the position of General Manager. Since we need a person who can "hit the ground running," we have selected a candidate who's had twelve years' experience in the industry. We are sure that with your excellent background you will find just the right position. |
| | No: | Your application for the position of General Manager has been rejected. We have found someone with better qualifications. |

| Positive Tone | Yes: | "I'm glad to tell you that your shipment will be sent on January 3." |
| | No: | "Unfortunately, your shipment won't be sent until January 3." |

| | Yes: | "Thank you for your suggestions about our prices. We do believe, however, that our prices are in line with those of our competitors." |
| | No: | "Your letter complaining about our prices was wrong. We are definitely in line with those of our competitors." |

| *You* Approach | Yes: | "You can be assured that . . . " |
| | No: | "I can assure you . . ." |

| Empathy | | "I certainly understand your concerns." |

After your letter is written, re-read it for the psychological impact. Is your message clear? Is it written in a natural, courteous, friendly, and sincere tone?

Word Selection

When you are speaking to someone face to face, much of what is said will be interpreted through nonverbal cues (gestures, voice, eye contact, movements, etc.). This is not possible via the written word; therefore, your choice of words is critical. Written communication is a powerful tool in that it provides a permanent record of what has been said.

Use Positive Words

Keep the words . . .	Not . . .
positive	negative
simple	complex
concise	excessive
conversational	trite
specific	general

The following are just a few of the words that communicate a positive message:

bonus	congratulations	convenient	excellent
delighted	friend	generous	glad
honest	immediately	I will	of course
pleasant	pleasure	pleasing	qualified
right	safe	sale	satisfactory
thank you	vacation	yes	

Active v. Passive Voice

Use the active voice in most situations. The active voice is the one in which the subject plays an active role; therefore, it is direct and lively. In the passive voice, the subject plays a passive role. The passive voice does have a place in letter writing, though. It can be used to emphasize a key word in a sentence by making it the subject (The shot was heard 'round the world.). Notice the differences in the sentences below.

Active	*Passive*
I will always remember my visit to Mexico.	My visit to Mexico will always be remembered by me.
The secretary typed the letter.	The letter was typed by the secretary.
Jim inspected the circuit boards.	The circuit boards were inspected by Jim.
The president authorized the checks.	The checks were authorized by the president.
Please turn off the lights before you leave. (*"You" is understood.*)	The lights should be turned off before you leave.

Building on Words

Writing is the process of building on words. There are several steps between the words and a coherent message.

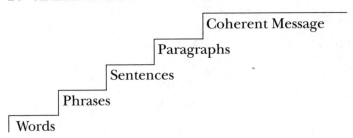

Keep It Short and Simple

> Perhaps the shortest letter ever written that most effectively expressed the writer's intentions was the one received by Victor Hugo from his publisher on February 26, 1802. Mr. Hugo wrote to his publisher asking how he liked the manuscript *Les Misérables.*
>
> The publisher responded as follows:
>
> " **!** "

> Gentlemen:
>
> You have undertaken to cheat me. I won't sue you for the law is too slow. I'll ruin you.
>
> Yours truly,
>
> *Cornelius Vanderbilt*

Both of the above letters are short and simple, yet incredibly powerful.

Notice the difference in the following two paragraphs. The message is clearer when many of the unnecessary words are removed.

No: I would greatly appreciate any ideas or suggestions that you would like to offer and assure you that each of your ideas will be given our strongest consideration and our fullest attention.

Yes: Please send us your ideas. They will be given our full consideration.

Many expressions that were considered trendy years ago are no longer fashionable. The following are substitutes for some expressions you should avoid:

Use	Avoid
allows	allows the opportunity
appeared	put in an appearance
as you asked	pursuant to your request
as you requested	pursuant to your request
as soon as	at the earliest possible date
because	due to the fact, inasmuch as
because of	in view of the fact that
concluded	arrived at the conclusion
consider	take under advisement
costs $100	costs a total of $100
delay	hold in abeyance
do	take appropriate measures
enclosed is	enclosed herewith please find
find out	ascertain
have	are in receipt of
I shall appreciate (Never thank someone in advance.)	thanking you in advance
if	in the event of
in March	during the month of March
in the future	at a future time
know	are fully cognizant
met	held a meeting
now	at the present time
payment	remuneration
regardless	irregardless (no such word)
separately	under separate cover
soon	in the near future
study (read)	peruse
thank you	I wish to take this opportunity to thank you
to provide	for the purpose of providing
try	endeavor
until you can	until such time as you can

Writing Styles

Another factor to consider in selecting your words is style. Styles generally fall into three categories: *formal, chatty,* and *personable.* Formal can sound stuffy and stilted, and chatty has a tendency to be too casual. The recommended style is personable because you can sound as if you are talking rather than writing and still maintain a professional quality. Take a look at the following examples:

Formal	I am writing with reference to your kind invitation to address the New York chapter of the American Spiritual Association. I appreciate your regard for my expertise. However, it is with deep regret that I must decline your kind invitation.
Chatty	Many thanks for the invite to chat with the American Spiritual Association. Sorry—can't make it. Have to be on the West Coast then.
Personable	Thank you for asking me to speak at the New York chapter of the American Spiritual Association. I would very much like to accept the invitation, but I must be on the West Coast that week.

Checklist

☑   Purpose was clearly stated.

☑   Psychological considerations were thought through.

☑   All the key points were logically included.

☑   Wrote naturally. (Talked—didn't write.)

☑   Projected a positive attitude.

☑   Addressed the reader's viewpoint—YOU.

☑   Complimented only when it was earned.

☑   Avoided slang and jargon.

☑   Was alert to word associations.

☑   Checked all numbers and spellings.

☑   Checked the overall appearance.

STATIONERY

We have already discussed parts, placement, and style; and organization, tone, and word selection. They fall in the category of mechanics. In addition to the mechanics of a letter, we must consider stationery. A business letter—much like a person—is judged by appearance, and the stationery would be the equivalent of the clothes you wear. A letter is often the first impression a reader gets of you and your company. And the overall effect of a letter can decide whether or not the letter achieves its purpose.

Quality

Bond paper is used for most business correspondence. It comes in several weights, the most common of which are 16-, 20-, and 24-pound bond. (The weight is determined by the weight of four $8\frac{1}{2}$ by 11 reams. Therefore, the higher the number, the thicker the paper.) Bond paper is available with a rag content that is determined by percentages—the most common of which is 25 percent rag. (The rag content is determined by the amount of rag lint in the paper. Therefore, the higher the rag content, the higher the quality and the price.)

Size

The standard size for business stationery is $8\frac{1}{2}$ by 11 inches (or 210 by 297 millimeters, in metric measurements). Baronial size, which measures $5\frac{1}{2}$ by $8\frac{1}{2}$ inches, is appropriate for personal business correspondence. Monarch size, which measures $7\frac{1}{4}$ by $10\frac{1}{2}$ inches, is often used by executives. You must remember, however, that paper smaller than the standard size of $8\frac{1}{2}$ by 11 inches is harder to find in a file drawer.

Color

White has been and continues to be the standard color for professional stationery. There are many variations of white (e.g., buff, ivory, cream, pale gray, etc.) which are being used more frequently. Colored stationery should be reserved for the glamour industries.

Letterhead

The hallmark of today's letterhead is simplicity. Years ago, stationery was excessively designed with the founding fathers and a listing of the product line often highlighted. The primary purpose of letterhead is to identify you and let the reader know how to get in touch with you. Therefore, letterhead should include the following:

• company name

• address

• telephone number

• fax number

Some letterhead contains the name of the president or key people in the company. And if your company has a logo, that should also be prominent.

When letterhead is being designed, the image of the company should be kept in mind. For example, a lawyer's stationery should have a much more sedate appearance than a graphic designer's. Start paying attention to letterheads you receive.

Second Sheets

The second sheet of a letter must match the first page in quality and color. The only difference between the first and second sheets is that the first sheet bears the letterhead and the second is blank.

Envelopes

No. 10 is the standard size for envelopes that enclose $8\frac{1}{2}$ by 11 inch stationery. If your company uses a smaller size stationery, the envelopes should be sized accordingly. Like second sheets, the envelopes must match the stationery in quality and color. A company usually orders envelopes at the same time it orders the stationery.

The company name and return address should appear in the upper-left corner on the face of the envelope. The font (type style) should match the letterhead.

GETTING CREATIVE

If you are using a computer, take advantage of electronic clip art. Electronic clip art is a collection of drawings and illustrations—public domain and copyright free. Of course, clip art isn't appropriate for all types of letters, but in certain cases illustrations do lend an appealing touch. The following are just a few of the thousands of electronic clip art illustrations that are available and how you might use them.

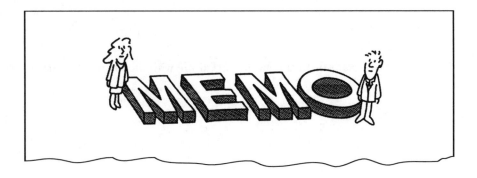

SHADOW BOX

DOUBLE BOX

You can search
the world over
and never
find . . .

MEMO

Note: All the illustrations in this book were done with electronic clip art.

PART · II

PRACTICAL GUIDE

CHAPTER THREE

EMPLOYMENT

In the course of your professional career, you will have occasion to write a variety of letters that relate to employment. Statistics have shown that Americans have two or three careers within a lifetime and change jobs periodically. Therefore, an application letter should be part of your repertoire. Additionally, you will undoubtedly be called upon to write a variety of letters or memos that deal with employment issues. The employment letters this chapter will focus on are:

- application
- acknowledging receipt of resume
- broadcast
- thank you
- formal job offer
- recommendation
- introducing new employee
- resignation

APPLICATION LETTER

An application letter must accompany each resume you send; therefore, it is one of the most important letters you will ever write. (If you are using a computer, it would be wise to prepare a boilerplate letter that can be adapted for each situation. That will save you the trouble of starting from scratch each time.) A well-written application letter can launch an interview and determine the course of your professional career. As you might have guessed, an application letter is not easy to write. Therefore, this chapter will carefully review the process. It takes thought and planning, but the time invested will be well worth the effort.

Let Your Personality Shine

Do not use someone else's application letter, no matter how wonderful and successful it might have been. Write a letter in your own style. Wouldn't an employer be disappointed if he or she met you and found that you were an entirely different person from the one who wrote the letter? An application letter should reflect *your* personality and *your* attitude toward your work and life. Use the examples in this book and others as guidelines.

Letterhead

If you are using a computer or have access to one, you can add a professional touch to your letters by preparing letterhead. The letterhead can be stored in the computer's memory and used each time you send out an application letter. The letterhead does not have to be fancy or elaborate.

EXAMPLES:

LORRAINE N. HAROLD
217 Woodholly Avenue, Dallas, TX 75208   (214) 962-4567

LORRAINE N. HAROLD
217 Woodholly Avenue
Dallas, TX 75208
(214) 962-4567

Helpful Hints

- Direct your letter to an individual by name and title whenever possible. There are many resources that can help you find this information. The company's receptionist might provide the names and titles you need. Or visit your local library.

- Keep the letter fairly short—generally three paragraphs.

- Do not reiterate all the information in your resume. Select the highlights and qualifications which best *sell you.*

- Emphasize the contribution you can make to the company.

- Avoid egotistical or trite remarks such as, "I have a good personality," "I am dependable," etc.

- It is okay to use "I" several times throughout the letter; after all the letter is about you. But do try to inject "you" into the letter whenever you can.

- Mention that your resume is enclosed or attached.

Opening Paragraph

Create an interesting opening paragraph that identifies your source (e.g., newspaper advertisement, personal contact, or direct solicitation). This paragraph must get the reader's attention. You have a very short time in which to make an initial impression so the reader will want to continue reading.

EXAMPLES:

Advertisement	Your advertisement for an Executive Secretary in THE BOSTON GLOBE is of great interest to me. I have an Associates Degree in Administration and would like to continue my career in the travel field.
Personal Contact	Mr. Eric Laurence, of your Contract Department, brought to my attention your need for a top-quality Contracts Administrator. Mr. Laurence is confident that my background and experience would enable me to meet all your requirements.

Direct Solicitation   As a recent college graduate certified in mathematics, I would like the opportunity to make a
contribution to the growth and high standards
of Spring Valley High School.

Convincing Middle Paragraph(s)

Elaborate on your qualifications and explain how they can serve the
company. Try to point out how you can do a better job for the company because of lessons you have learned in school or on the job.

EXAMPLES:

> My background includes 15 years of experience in manufacturing
> and engineering. I am experienced in the construction of
> production machinery and plant engineering requirements. I
> have been praised for my ability to direct and motivate others and
> have demonstrated the ability to meet very tight deadlines.

> For five years I was the Manager of Marketing Communications at
> Sterling Corporation. I managed a $3.5 million budget, against
> which I saved $750,000 in one year. My responsibilities included a
> broad range of assignments for international audiences, including
> sales and customer training, newsletters, product brochures,
> advertising, news releases, user documentation, and video
> productions.

> My employment with A&B Life Insurance Company and Delta
> Mutual Insurance Company taught me a great deal about human
> relations and the finer techniques of selling. As a result of this
> experience, I am convinced that I can build sales and goodwill for
> [company name].

Closing Paragraph

Request an interview, and include a telephone number where you can be reached. It is not necessary to repeat the phone number if you're using a prepared letterhead that has the number.

EXAMPLES:

> I would welcome the opportunity to meet with you so that you can evaluate the enthusiastic and creative contributions I can make to [company name]. You can reach me at (000) 000-0000 any afternoon after two o'clock.

> Enclosed is a copy of my resume. As you will see, my background closely matches your job description. Please call me at (000) 000-0000 so we can arrange for a personal interview.

> I am willing to travel and would be more than willing to relocate. Please call me at the number above (assuming it is on the letterhead) so that we can discuss how my qualifications can be of benefit to [company name].

Salary Requirements

Salary requirements *are not* addressed in a letter; they are addressed at the interview. However, if you are responding to an ad that asks for your salary requirements, how blunt should you be?

1. Ignore it completely.

2. Mention the range.

3. Give your current salary.

4. State that you expect a salary commensurate with your experience and with the responsibilities of the job for which you are applying.

This is somewhat like a multiple-choice test, only there is no correct answer. The experts vary in their opinions, so go with the option with which you are most comfortable.

Check Your Letter

☑ Have you applied the principles of effective writing?

☑ Will the opening paragraph convince the reader to want to know more?

☑ Did you make it clear that you understand the requirements for the position?

☑ Did you indicate that you are interested in what you can do for the company?

☑ Did you mention that you are enclosing your resume?

☑ Does the final paragraph request an interview or other specific action?

11 Planter Street
Salem, MA 01970
January 15, 19—

Ms. Beth Wolf, President
Steven & David, Inc.
11 Nancy Ann Street
Woburn, MA 01801

Dear Ms. Wolf:

Re: Position of Principal Engineer

Ms. Kristen N. Michael, Manager of your Finance Department, mentioned that you are seeking a Principal Engineer for your new product line. She suggested that I contact you.

My twenty-five years of engineering experience in advanced systems design has earned me the following recognition, which I am certain will be of benefit to your company:

- Excalibur Award, Textron's highest honor, for leadership in MK 21 Fuze Product that enhanced the yield by 100% on major production contract.

- Textron's individual recognition award for outstanding contribution in a lead engineering position in a military satellite program.

- Patent pending for high-speed camera scoring, a project which was displayed at the Pentagon and Picatinny Arsenal.

- Special recognition from Center of Astrophysics for major contribution to Einstein (HEAO-2) project, a high-energy satellite telescope for deep space observation.

After you have had a chance to review the enclosed resume, I would appreciate the opportunity to come in for an interview. I will call you early next week to arrange for such a meeting. Thank you.

Sincerely,

Robert W. Littlehale

Enclosure

2 Column Street
Chicago, IL 60657
October 30, 19—

Mr. James Haskell
3 Amesbury Street
Chicago, IL 60657

Dear Mr. Haskell:

Would your company benefit from the services of a creative, innovative technical writer? My contributions to former companies have resulted in increased sales and an enhanced company image through the production of easy-to-read user manuals. I can make that same contribution to [company name].

I used my English degree from Northeastern University to launch my technical writing career more than ten years ago. Since then I have written articles in several professional magazines and have written more than 15 user manuals for both technical and non-technical audiences.

Please give me the opportunity to meet with you to discuss any permanent or freelance jobs that may be available. I will bring my portfolio so that you can evaluate my writing style. Please call me at (000) 000-0000.

Very truly yours,

Donna Randall

Cleo N. George

2 Union Lane, Salem, MA 01970
(508) 123-4567

April 8, 19—

Ms. Becki Gentry
Malcolm-Ed Technology, Inc.
357 Avon Street
Suffern, NY 10901

Dear Ms. Gentry:

I read with interest your advertisement in the Sunday edition of THE
NEW YORK TIMES describing positions in Process Engineering and
Material Science. As you will see from my enclosed resume, I have the
applicable experience and education.

In ten years of process engineering management at Seriglio Company, I
was responsible for developing the metalization processes for several
generations of integrated circuit technologies. My most significant
challenge there was the successful management of the creativity that
goes into advanced development. At Atlas Research Corporation, I
focused that creativity into the development of the aluminum
planarization process for the Hercules sputtering system. This work
enabled sputtered metalization to meet the needs of submicron
interconnect technologies.

If you need further information, please feel free to contact me at
(000) 000-0000. I will call you within the next two weeks to discuss my
qualifications in more detail.

Sincerely,

Cleo N. George

Enc.

ACKNOWLEDGING RECEIPT
OF RESUME

Malcolm-Ed Technology

This is to acknowledge receipt of your resume for the positions in Process Engineering and Material Science. We've had an overwhelming response to our advertisement, and you can be assured that each resume will be given careful consideration.

Once this process has been completed, we will contact each candidate whose background matches our needs. Thank you for considering the Malcolm-Ed Company.

Human Resources Manager

Marck²

100 Market Street
San Francisco, CA 94117
(415) 353-4557

June 26, 19—

Mr. Marc Alan
50 Parade Route
Reno, NV 89515

Dear Mr. Alan:

Thank you for your recent application to Marck².

Although your resume is very impressive, we have received resumes from people whose backgrounds more closely match our needs. We will, however, keep your resume on file in the event that a suitable position should become available.

Good luck in your job search.

Sincerely,

Mark W. Schreier

BROADCAST LETTER

A broadcast letter is similar in style and content to an application letter. The difference is that it is sent *instead of* a resume, so it should contain all the information you want the reader to know. It is not necessary to limit a broadcast letter to one page. The broadcast letter is becoming more popular as the job market becomes more competitive, and people want their letters to be noticed.

If you are sending a broadcast letter, prepare at least three bulleted items that best sell your professional strengths and accomplishments. In certain industries, it might be appropriate to quantify your accomplishments.

EXAMPLES:

- Saved $750,000 the first year.

- Supervised a staff of 20, with 4 direct reports.

- Increased sales by 17% in the first quarter.

- Managed a $2.5 million budget.

The purpose of this section is not to endorse a broadcast letter over an application letter; it is merely to let you know there are options.

Notice the difference between this letter and the one written by Cleo N. George in the Application Letter section.

Cleo N. George
2 Union Lane, Salem, MA 01970
(508) 123-4567

April 8, 19—

Ms. Becki Gentry
Malcolm-Ed Technology, Inc.
357 Avon Street
Suffern, NY 10901

Dear Ms. Gentry:

Your most vital link with the customer is made through applications. It is here that a combination of technical expertise, salesmanship, and communications ability will connect your customers with the performance of your product. I have provided this combination with two major equipment suppliers over the last seven years and would like the opportunity to do the same for you at Malcolm-Ed Technology.

- At Atlas Research Corporation, I managed their Applications Lab for the Hercules sputtering system. I brought my technical expertise to bear on this new product and developed processes to provide successful demonstrations within a few months.

- At AER Corporation, I built up their Applications Lab from a single prototype Apollo sputter system and one engineer, to a modern, clean facility with three production-level systems and a staff of five engineers. With aluminum and titanium nitride processes developed under my leadership, successful customer demonstrations and follow-up on customer support made the Apollo the market leader.

- An additional twelve years of process engineering experience in the semiconductor wafer fabrication industry has provided me with a firm background in a variety of deposition and etching processes.

With this background and a history of successful management of process labs, I can help your Applications Lab put your product into market leadership. I would be glad to discuss further details of my experience at a personal interview.

Sincerely,

Cleo N. George

Enc.

THANK-YOU LETTER

After the interview, take the time to write a thank-you or follow-up letter expressing appreciation for the interview and your interest in the position. The tone should be one of sincerity and enthusiasm. Some executive recruiters suggest a hand-written letter, but a type-written letter is still the convention. Your letter should include the following:

- your appreciation for the interview

- something you did not get a chance to tell the interviewer and/ or a reiteration of one of your accomplishments which impressed the interviewer

- your desire to work for the company

August 15, 19—

Ms. Debra Hahn
Mikedrew Brothers
11 Kenneth Street
El Dorado, AR 71730

Dear Ms. Hahn:

I very much enjoyed our meeting this afternoon to discuss the opportunity of Manager of Desktop Publishing.

The chance to champion desktop publishing in the context of Mikedrew's environment is especially intriguing. I'm sure that the combination of my expertise and your needs would give your new Manager an opportunity to make an immediate contribution.

I look forward to returning for my next interview with the hope of sharing my enthusiasm and talents with Mikedrew Brothers.

Sincerely,

Bailey Phelps

FORMAL JOB OFFER

Formal job offers are generally written, not verbal, so there will be no misunderstanding as to the terms and conditions. Formal job offers generally have a place on the bottom of the letter where the applicant can indicate his/her acceptance of the terms.

Formal job offers should include:

- salary, bonus plan, etc.

- relocation benefits, if applicable

- vacation and holiday policies

- insurance benefits

- anticipated starting date

FORMAL JOB REJECTION

A job rejection is, of course, more difficult to write because no one likes to be the bearer of bad news. When you think of the number of candidates who are generally interviewed for one position, you will realize that this letter is written more often than one extending an offer. *It is a good idea not to reject any viable candidates until the one you have selected has accepted the position, on the chance that he/she declines the offer.*

Formal job rejections should include:

- praise for the candidate's credentials

- your regrets

- best wishes for future employment

Jay N. Robin Corporation
5 Logwood Circle, Burlington, VT 00000
(802) 123-4567

January 15, 19—

Mr. Gerald Sullivan
3 Thomas Circle
Essex Junction, VT 00000

Dear Mr. Sullivan:

Jay N. Robin Corporation is very pleased to offer you the position of Director of Human Resources, reporting to Lynne McDonough. Your starting salary will be $6,500 per month plus an incentive plan for your first two years of employment. The plan will be based on job performance as defined by objectives to be developed between you and Lynne McDonough. The plan will provide a target payout of $6,000 per year in February of each of the appropriate years.

Your relocation benefits will include packing, moving, and unpacking of all household belongings. As I described, we will provide a hotel room or an efficiency apartment for you and your family for up to three months to afford you an opportunity to find a permanent residence.

The first ninety days of employment will be considered an orientation period. Written performance reviews are received on an annual basis. The enclosed packet will outline many of Jay N. Robin's benefits, including health, dental, life, and disability. In addition to those benefits, we offer twelve paid holidays and ten days of vacation per year.

Please indicate your acceptance of this employment by signing the bottom of this letter and returning a copy to me by January 21, 19—. We welcome you to Jay N. Robin Corporation and look forward to working with you. If you have any questions, please call me at extension 1234.

Sincerely,

Jay N. Robin, President

_____   _____

Signature   Date

Jay N. Robin Corporation
5 Logwood Circle, Burlington, VT 00000
(802) 123-4567

January 29, 19—

Ms. Amy Dober
12 Dickerson Street
Burlington, VT 00000

Dear Ms. Dober:

It was delightful meeting with you on all three occasions when you interviewed for the position of Director of Human Resources. You certainly have an impressive background.

We have, unfortunately, selected a candidate whose background more closely matches our needs. You were a very viable candidate, and we wish you success in finding a new position.

Sincerely,

Jay N. Robin, President

RECOMMENDATION LETTER

A word of caution: Be wary of giving out any information about an employee or former employee that is less than favorable. We have become a very litigious society and a number of employers have been sued for making unfavorable remarks. It is for this reason that many companies have adopted a policy of merely verifying a person's employment and length of employment.

If you should be asked to have your name used as a reference and you do not feel that you can honestly give a favorable recommendation, you would be wise to decline. However, if circumstances force you to terminate a valued employee, the employee may ask for a letter of recommendation to take with him/her. That is very appropriate and often done.

When you are responding to a written request for information about a former employee, be certain to mark the response "Confidential." The reply should outline facts about the employee that will give a new employer an accurate picture. Try to separate opinions from facts.

Fact: Ms. Lavin took charge of the smooth running of our office and was always professional in her approach. She is an excellent secretary.

Opinion: Ms. Lavin will make an excellent secretary.

Letters of recommendation should paint an accurate picture of the employee and should include:

- employee's position or job title while in your employ

- major contributions or admirable qualities

- reason(s) for release, provided they are not negative.

May 1, 19—

CONFIDENTIAL

Mr. A. L. Duran, President
A. L. Duran, Inc.
204 Iguana Street
Cleveland, OH 44197-8032

Dear Mr. Duran:

In response to your letter of April 22, Miche Grenier joined A.L. Duran, Inc., in June 19—. At that time, the company was expanding and had just entered into a major contract. This contract required the complete rewriting of an extensive user manual for our primary software product. Although he was given no time to become familiar with the software, Mr. Grenier produced a professional manual on time for our customer.

Mr. Grenier also wrote and redesigned almost all of our published materials, including its market literature, which enhanced the company image. He took initiative in several efforts, such as writing articles featuring the company, preparing press releases, and developing a list of contacts among industry publishers.

Unfortunately, sales have suffered from the recession, and we have had to reduce our staff dramatically. While we regret the loss of Mr. Grenier, it is a step that has been forced upon us.

I recommend him highly as an experienced and motivated professional.

Sincerely,

A. L. Duran, President

INTRODUCING A NEW EMPLOYEE

Some employees join companies and go virtually unnoticed. It makes a new employee feel welcome when a notice is sent around and/or placed in a bulletin board introducing him or her. This can be in the form of a memo and should include:

- name
- position
- short bio
- starting date

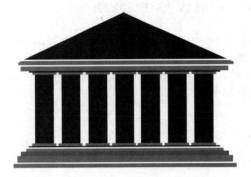

A-Z Custom Designs

957 Hayes Street

San Francisco, CA 94117

(415) 123-4567

Date: October 2, 19—
To: All Staff Members
From: Mike Della Selva, Vice President

Marc Alan will be joining our company on October 9. Marc brings to our company ten years of experience in the field of architecture. He has a degree from Georgia Tech and a background in custom-designed housing. One of Marc's designs was featured in the June edition of ARCHITECT'S DIGEST. Marc will be a welcome addition to our distinguished staff.

Please join me in extending Marc a cordial welcome.

RESIGNATION LETTER

Always resign a position without creating hard feelings. Therefore, present your intention to leave in a positive way. Even if you feel the company did not treat you fairly, and you were forced to look for a new job, present a positive tone. A resignation letter should include:

- effective date

- last day you will report to work

- your willingness to train your successor

- expression of success for the company's future

Date: February 9, 19—

To: Lloyd Perell

From: Olga Andrew

cc: Elizabeth N. Michael

I am hereby submitting my resignation from Roberts & Sons, Inc., effective on the above date. My last working day will be February 23.

My tenure at Roberts & Sons has been enjoyable, and I have been fortunate to work with capable and dedicated people. I have, in turn, performed to the best of my ability.

At this time, for the benefit of my family and my career, I have formally accepted a new position in another company. I will be more than happy to train my successor to insure a smooth transition.

Thank you for your past consideration. I wish you every success.

CHAPTER FOUR

CREDIT AND COLLECTION

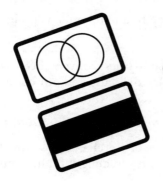

Charge it!

CREDIT

Credit has become a way of life. It is estimated that nearly 90 percent of all the buying and selling in the United States is done on a credit basis. Charge accounts flourish; businesses burgeon; and the mail carrier collapses under the weight of the end-of-the-month billings that greet customers each month.

Credit is advantageous for consumers because they can buy now and pay later, avoid carrying large amounts of cash, and exchange or return merchandise more easily. Businesses obviously profit from higher sales, but they do experience a down side. Credit increases their cost of doing business; capital is tied up; and there are losses from bad debts. Therefore, businesses must be cautious and not extend credit to every customer who requests it. Credit is based on the 4-Cs:

Character	a sense of dealing honestly and ethically
Capacity	the ability to pay
Capital	tangible assets
Conditions	business trends or demands

Soliciting Customers

Businesses cannot rely on walk-in customers to supply an ample base of qualified charge customers, so they solicit. Solicitation can be in the form of a general mailing, welcoming a new family to town, announcing a store celebration or seasonal sale. The letter should:

- *Project a courteous and friendly welcome.*

- *Extend an invitation to come in and browse* (or in the case of a larger business, to contact you) *and to fill out a credit application.*

    When you come in, please stop by and fill out an application for a charge account.

    Won't you give me a call at your earliest convenience so that we can arrange to meet personally to discuss how our credit arrangements can serve you.

- *Entice the customer with information about your merchandise or services.*

    [Company] has a treasure trove of merchandise waiting for you. We hope you'll stop by to browse and delight in the unusual merchandise you'll find.

    You'll continue to enjoy these exclusive advantages that are unavailable to other shoppers:

    - Courtesy Certificates to create your own sales.
    - Previews of sales and exclusive storewide events.
    - A 90-day 0% finance charge.

- *Stress the advantages of buying on credit.*

    It's so much easier to shop when you can write a check just once a month.

- *Urge action.*

    We know that you'll enjoy the privilege and convenience of being a [company name] charge customer. Why not stop by soon and let us serve you?

    A typical letter of solicitation might read as follows on the next page.

M ARRIC BROTHERS

24 Besen Parkway, Monsey, NY 10952
(914) 352-8198

May 10, 19—

Mr. Frank Lindsell
The Jimmy Store
36 Deborah Lane
Spring Valley, NY 10977

Dear Mr. Lindsell:

Congratulations in having succeeded in managing your credit so wisely. It's for that reason that you've been selected as a candidate for our valuable Marric Brothers Credit Card. Here's how the Marric Brothers Credit Card can save you money:

☑ *Low interest rates and cash advances.* With an 11.8% variable APR, your credit card can save you many percentage points over other cards. In fact, this is one of the few cards available today to offer such a low APR on both purchases and cash advances.

☑ *No annual fees.* While some low APR cards look good at first glance, beware of the fine print. Annual fees can be as high as $50 per year. With ours— there is never an annual fee.

☑ *Sizable credit line.* You'll hold a powerful credit line of up to $2,500. A Marric Brothers Credit Card lets you take your total available credit line in cash for any reason you choose.

☑ *Grace period for purchases.* Some lenders charge interest immediately on the amount of your purchases. Not us. We allow you a 30-day, interest-free grace period for payment on purchases.

☑ *Special privileges.* You'll be notified of advance sales and private sales that are exclusively for credit customers.

Just fill out the enclosed credit application today and enjoy the advantages that the Marric Brothers Credit Card has to offer.

Sincerely,

Marc N. Eric
Credit Manager

el

Extending Credit Privileges

Let us assume that a credit check has revealed the customer to be *credit worthy*. The first step in establishing the credit relationship is to send a "good news" letter extending credit privileges. The letter should:

- *Approve the credit cheerfully.*

  Welcome to our family of satisfied customers who come into [company] and say, "Charge it!"

  On behalf of everyone at [company], I'd like to thank you for your trust and loyalty.

- *Explain specific terms of the account.* (This portion should be embedded in the middle of the letter because it detracts from the friendly tone. However, it is necessary information.)

- *Encourage more buying.*

  The catalog contains several order forms and return envelopes that will make it easy for you to order from [company name].

- *Express appreciation for customer's patronage, encourage open communication, and/or discuss company services.*

  Our sales representative, Morty Teisch, will be in your area next week. He would like to schedule an appointment to tell you how we can cooperate with your dealers in national and international advertising. At that time, he'll be delighted to answer any questions you may have.

  At [company] we regard you as our top priority. We look forward to serving you as our customer for years to come.

A typical letter extending credit privileges might read as follows on the next page.

Marric brothers

24 Besen Parkway, Monsey, NY 10952
(914) 352-8198

June 15, 19—

Mr. Frank Lindsell
The Jimmy Store
36 Deborah Lane
Spring Valley, NY 10977

Dear Mr. Lindsell:

Welcome! We are pleased to present your new Marric Brothers Credit Card—your entree to a world of special privileges reserved exclusively for you. You can be sure that our sales associates will do everything possible to make shopping at Marric Brothers a pleasant and satisfying experience. If you have any special needs—just ask!

Starting now, you will be invited to attend private sales and enjoy savings that are not advertised to the general public. You will be notified by mail in advance of selected sales in all your favorite Marric Brothers locations—from fashions to home furnishings and much more.

We look forward to seeing you at Marric Brothers where the exciting world of shopping awaits you!

Sincerely,

Marc N. Eric
Credit Manager

el

Refusing Credit Privileges

Let us assume that a credit check has revealed the customer is not *credit worthy*. The intention of this letter is to convince the customer to deal with you on a cash basis, not to discourage buying. Tell the customer you are unable to extend credit right now, but leave the door open. The letter should:

- *Express appreciation for the customer's interest in the company.*

  Thank you for requesting credit with [company name]. And thank you for completing and returning your application forms so quickly.

- *Refuse by first mentioning favorable observations and ending with a refusal of credit.*

  Your references unanimously agreed that you are one of their most cooperative customers. After carefully reviewing your many obligations, however, we feel that we cannot open a credit account for you at this time. While you are working through your obligations, however, we can still be of service to you.

- *Offer alternatives such as reapplying at a later date and buying on a cash basis in the meantime.*

  In the meantime, we'd be delighted to fill your orders on a cash basis and to review your credit request as soon as some of your obligations have been satisfied.

- *Assure the person you want their business and are willing to work with him/her.*

- *Sound sincere, not degrading.*

  A typical letter refusing credit privileges might read as follows on the next page.

M ARRIC BROTHERS

24 Besen Parkway, Monsey, NY 10952
(914) 352-8198

August 12, 19—

Mr. Otto Mann
7 Inland Road
Suffern, NY 10901

Dear Mr. Mann:

We thank you for your request for credit with Marric Brothers; it is a compliment to us. Your references have all agreed that you have been very cooperative and are always willing to discuss the details of your account.

Our experience has taught us that next to credit references, the most important aspect affecting business success is cash on hand. This is especially true for new businesses such as yours. We always encourage our customers to maintain a cash balance that will allow them to sufficiently cover salaries and expenses for at least six months. We are certain that within the next few months you will be able to increase your average cash balance. It is, therefore, for your benefit as well as ours, that we suggest that you reapply for credit when your cash position is somewhat stronger.

Enclosed you will find our latest sales brochure. You will notice that an additional 5 percent discount is offered to any customer who pays by cash. Just fill out the order blank, enclose your check, and your order will be on its way.

We will be more than happy to review your credit request in the near future and look forward to having you join our family of satisfied customers.

Sincerely,

Marc N. Eric
Credit Manager

el

Encourage Credit Buying

The purpose of extending credit to customers is to increase sales. Therefore, an active account is an advantage to the customer and the business. If an account goes unused for an extended period of time, ask yourself these questions: If I were a credit customer . . .

- What would it take for me to reactivate my account?

- Would I like to hear, "We miss you"?

- Is there something special waiting for me?

- Is there is a store celebration or seasonal sale?

Do not over-emphasize "use your credit." Your letter must express an appreciation for the customer's business.

A typical letter encouraging credit buying might read as follows on the next page.

Marric Brothers

24 Besen Parkway, Monsey, NY 10952
(914) 352-8198

September 30, 19—

Mr. Frank Lindsell
The Jimmy Store
36 Deborah Lane
Spring Valley, NY 10977

Dear Mr. Lindsell:

We at Marric Brothers greatly appreciate your patronage and your prompt payments of your monthly statements. You should be proud, Mr. Lindsell, of your fine credit record.

It is a pleasure to have you as one of our valued customers, and we want to continue giving you the kind of service you deserve. Why not stop by to take advantage of the special once-a-year inventory sale that will be offered during the week of July 1st. We are here to help you whenever you visit us.

Sincerely,

Marc N. Eric
Credit Manager

el

COLLECTION

It is important to establish a working rapport with a customer as soon as an account is opened. Some companies send thank you letters to customers who pay on time; others offer them cash discounts. There are some people and/or companies, however, who are remiss in their financial obligations for a variety of reasons. Excuses for not paying bills are as varied as people themselves. They range from "I've run out of checks and the printers are on strike" to "I'm in jail and will pay you in two years when I get out." There was even an individual who placed his own obituary in the newspaper and mailed a copy to all his creditors.

Credit managers, or people who deal with debtors on a regular basis, realize that the longer an account is outstanding, the less likely it is to be paid. Also, the sooner the customer pays the bill, the sooner that customer will make additional purchases. So it behooves everyone to settle an account quickly.

Collection letters are generally written in a series, ranging from gentle reminders to the threat of turning the matter over to a collection agency. This section will address the following letters:

1. Gentle Reminder
2. Stronger Reminder
3. Request for an Explanation
4. Appeal for Payment
5. Last Call for Payment

Gentle Reminder

It is quite possible that this reminder and the payment will cross in the mail. Or perhaps the customer just forgot. The gentle reminder may be a preprinted card or letter, a sticker that is attached to the bill, or a note on the bottom of the second bill that is sent. The gentle reminder should:

* *Call attention to the oversight.*

    We haven't received payment for your last invoice. If it's on its way . . . thanks. If not, please send it out today.

- *Urge prompt payment.*

  Won't you drop your check in the mail today? A self-addressed envelope is enclosed for your convenience.

- *Suggest merchandise that may be of interest.*

  The prediction for this winter is cold and snowy. Have you considered purchasing a snow blower? [Company name] is offering a pre-season sale on ABC snow blowers during the next three weeks, or as long as the supply lasts. Once your account has been satisfied, wouldn't it be nice to know that you'll never have to shovel your driveway again?

  A typical gentle reminder might read as follows on page 68.

MARRIC BROTHERS

24 Besen Parkway, Monsey, NY 10952
(914) 352-8198

January 15, 19—

Mr. Frank Lindsell
The Jimmy Store
36 Deborah Lane
Spring Valley, NY 10977

Dear Mr. Lindsell:

Subject: Account No. 1234

We know that the due date of your payment probably had slipped your mind and that by now your check is already in the mail. If so, we thank you.

More helpful hints, such as the ones included in your recent shipment, are available to you upon request. If there is any other way that Marric Brothers can be helpful to you, please let us know.

Sincerely,

Marc N. Eric
Credit Manager

el

Stronger Reminder

Even your fast-paying customers might overlook a payment. If the gentle reminder goes unheeded, a stronger reminder should be sent the following month. The stronger reminder should:

- *Reaffirm the good relationship you've enjoyed.*

- *Stress the customer's financial obligation.*

- *Employ sales tactics.*

    When you mail your payment of $250, due April 5, why not send your summer order?

- *Offer to make payment easy.*

    Won't you slip your check into the self-addressed envelope that's enclosed?

    A typical stronger reminder might read as follows on page 70.

MARRIC BROTHERS

24 Besen Parkway, Monsey, NY 10952
(914) 352-8198

February 15, 19—

Mr. Frank Lindsell
The Jimmy Store
36 Deborah Lane
Spring Valley, NY 10977

Dear Mr. Lindsell:

Subject: Account No. 1234

You have always been one of our valued customers, and we look forward to being of service to you for many more years.

We know that you, as a businessperson yourself, appreciate those who meet their financial obligations in a timely manner. We do, too. Won't you please send us your check in the amount of $500 in the self-addressed envelope.

Within the next two weeks you will receive our catalog displaying our new line of winter merchandise. Our sales representative will call you shortly thereafter to help you determine your needs.

Sincerely,

Marc N. Eric
Credit Manager

el

Request for an Explanation

This third letter in the collection series is sent to customers who have ignored the previous reminders and who generally keep their accounts current. It assumes that something out of the ordinary has prevented the customer from making payment or offers to open the lines of communication. The letter should:

- *Request communication from the customer.*

    I would like to talk to you about the circumstances that have caused your bill in the amount of $1,000 to become three months overdue.

    Can you help us? We are wondering about the circumstances that have caused your bill in the amount of $500 to become three months overdue.

- *Suggest that perhaps there might be an error in the bill or some good reason for the delay.*

    You have always paid your bills so promptly that we are wondering if there might have been an error in the bill.

    Because you have always been such a fast-paying customer, we are wondering if there is some reason why you are unable to make full payment at this time.

- *Show sincere interest in settling the account.*

    Be assured that we will cooperate in any way we can. If you are having financial difficulties, we would be more than happy to work out an easy-payment plan.

- *Make it easy to respond.*

    An explanation? Your check for $670? A payment plan? Please put one of them in the self-addressed envelope today.

A typical request for an explanation letter might read as follows on page 72.

M ARRIC BROTHERS

24 Besen Parkway, Monsey, NY 10952
(914) 352-8198

March 15, 19—

Mr. Frank Lindsell
The Jimmy Store
36 Deborah Lane
Spring Valley, NY 10977

Dear Mr. Lindsell:

Subject: Account No. 1234

After three months, we still have not received your check in the amount of $500 or any explanation as to why your payment has not been sent. Since you have always paid so promptly, we are wondering if perhaps there are extenuating circumstances or if there is some error in your statement.

If either is the case, please contact us so that we can work together to retain your good credit standing. Or, place your check for $500 in the enclosed envelope.

Sincerely,

Marc N. Eric
Credit Manager

el

Appeal for Payment

Four months have passed, and it is now time to apply pressure. Never suggest that the customer pay because your company needs the money. Also, do not be sarcastic or insulting. Remember, you still want to retain the customer's business, if possible. The letter should:

- *Recap the history of the account.*

  Your account is now four months past due and you have ignored all our prior notices.

- *Appeal to the customer's pride or sense of fair play, or employ any psychological appeal you feel may work.*

  By sending your check today, you will be able to continue your fine credit reputation and continue to order without having to include a check each time.

- *Warn of further action.*

  You are putting your good credit reputation at risk. Please do not force us to take this matter further.

- *Indicate your faith in the customer's intention to pay.*

  We know you understand the importance of a good credit reputation. Why not put your check in the mail today, while it's fresh in your mind?

A typical appeal for payment letter might read as follows on page 74.

MARRIC BROTHERS

---

24 Besen Parkway, Monsey, NY 10952
(914) 352-8198

April 15, 19—

Mr. Frank Lindsell
The Jimmy Store
36 Deborah Lane
Spring Valley, NY 10977

Dear Mr. Lindsell:

Subject: Account No. 1234

Have you ever considered that your credit reputation is much like an insurance policy; it protects you against loss? The loss of buying on credit can be devastating to your business. It affects your cash flow, your ability to replenish your stock, and will cost you the goodwill you have worked so hard to establish.

Your account is now four months past due, and you have not responded to any of our correspondence. By sending your check in the amount of $500 today, you will ensure the privilege of maintaining the good credit reputation you now have. Take a moment now to drop your check in the mail.

Please do not make it necessary for us to take this matter further, because you are one of our valued customers.

Sincerely,

Marc N. Eric
Credit Manager

el

Last Call for Payment

Five months have passed, and you will make one last appeal. The customer has ignored all your efforts and you cannot afford to be patient any longer. The customer will be given one last opportunity to pay before this matter is turned over to an attorney or a collection agency. Even at this late date, you would like to salvage the relationship. The letter should:

- *Set a firm deadline—usually five to ten days.*

   If we don't receive payment in full within ten days from the date of this letter, this matter will be turned over to our attorneys for collection.

- *Outline the action you will take.*

   Do not make it necessary for us to take legal action. Put your check in the enclosed envelope and mail it today.

- *Stress the importance of a good credit reputation.*

   [Name], we have been more than fair. For the last five months you have ignored all our efforts to contact you. As an upstanding member of the business community, your credit reputation is of great value. You are now in danger of placing a permanent blemish on that reputation.

- *Offer a final chance for payment.*

   This is the last effort we will make to contact you directly. Please put your check in the mail today to avoid legal action.

A typical last call for payment letter might read as follows on page 76.

M ARRIC BROTHERS

24 Besen Parkway, Monsey, NY 10952
(914) 352-8198

May 15, 19—

Mr. Frank Lindsell
The Jimmy Store
36 Deborah Lane
Spring Valley, NY 10977

Dear Mr. Lindsell:

Subject: Account No. 1234

For five months we have been writing to you in an attempt to clear up your unpaid balance of $500. You have chosen to ignore all our efforts.

Can't we settle this matter between ourselves? If you send your check for $500 today, you can continue your good credit reputation. Unless payment in full is received within ten days from the date of this letter, we will turn this matter over for collection.

The choice is yours. If your check reaches us by May 25, your credit reputation will remain intact, and we will be able to continue doing business with you on a credit basis. Please mail us your check for $500 today.

Sincerely,

Marc N. Eric
Credit Manager

el

CHAPTER FIVE

CLAIMS AND ADJUSTMENTS

Once upon a time in the Land of Shoppers, every department store had a "Complaint Department." Disgruntled people would stand in line, waiting to tear the hair out of the poor person behind the counter.

Just what does the phrase *Complaint Department* conjure up? The word *complaint* connotes unpleasantness and negativism. Nowadays these same stores have *Customer Service Departments*. Isn't that presenting a better perception? The words *customer service* project a positive image—people behind the counters who are anxious to solve your problems. Along the same lines, years ago people wrote *complaint* letters; now they write *claim* letters.

Many companies welcome letters letting them know if something is wrong (in moderate numbers, of course). If the company does not know there is a problem, there is no opportunity to correct it. Businesses depend on satisfied customers.

CLAIMS

"Grin, don't grunt." In order to maintain the goodwill of customers, businesses *do* try to solve customer dissatisfaction quickly and fairly. When you are looking for an adjustment, remember the following:

1. *Timing is crucial.* Seek an adjustment as soon as the problem arises. You will weaken your claim by waiting too long.

2. *Always approach the right person.* Choose someone in the company who is in a position to act on your claim. It might be the Vice President of Sales or the Director of the Customer Service Department.

> A phone call to [name of business] indicated that you are the person whom I should contact.

> As Manager of [department] I'm certain you are the person to help me.

3. *Always act on the assumption that the business is anxious to right the wrong.* Do not argue or threaten. Avoid expressions like "Your product stinks."

> Yes: There is apparently a great deal of confusion about this account, and I hope that you will recheck your figures.
>
>   *-or-*
>
>   Over the last several years, every time I've visited [store], your salespeople have been extremely courteous. That is why I am so surprised.
>
> No: I did not think your HolidayGram was very funny . . . Your competitors offer better benefits and other advantages, so why should I bother with you?

4. *Present the details in logical order, offering as many facts and documents as possible.* Assume you will be treated fairly. Include a description of the original transaction and a clear explanation of your disappointment. Supply names, prices, and dates. Send copies of invoices, sales slips, canceled checks, or other relevant documentation that will validate your claim.

> On May 5, I purchased a leather sofa at your store. Enclosed is a copy of the invoice with all the information you should need. The sofa was delivered on June 15, and we have had it in our home for two months. Already, the webbing underneath has given way and the springs are starting to drop down.

> On October 12, I ordered a set of books from your store and charged them to my Visa account No. xx xx xxxx. The books were delivered yesterday, November 2. The outer wrappings appear to have been torn and mutilated, and the books were damaged.

5. *Let the reader know what adjustment would satisfy you.* If you are not sure, ask the reader to be fair. Or, no adjustment may be sought.

> I've checked the warranty, which guarantees the material and workmanship for one year. Therefore, please have someone call me as soon as possible so that we can arrange to have a new sofa delivered.

> I am returning the books in question via UPS. Please send me either a new set of books or credit my account.

> I was lucky. I took a handful of raisins, but there was no damage to my teeth or mouth. I would recommend that you keep an eye on what goes into your raisins. The stone, no worse for the wear, is enclosed for your scrutiny.

Merchandise Not Under Guarantee

There may be occasions when you are seeking an adjustment for merchandise that was never guaranteed or is no longer covered by the guarantee. Your job as a dissatisfied customer would be to convince the reader that he/she should accept responsibility and rectify the problem. In addition to outlining the details that would be included in a standard claim letter, it is important to establish a good reason why the company should accept the responsibility. It might be for general customer satisfaction, company reputation, etc.

> A long-time customer is a reliable customer, and I qualify on both counts. I've been coming to your store for more than ten years, and . . .

UP, UP, & AWAY TRAVEL
345 Glossard Street
Atlanta, GA 30332
(404) 545-6760

April 3, 19—

Able Tour Operators
Attention: Barbara Gillis
34 Journal Square
Pontotoc, TX 47456

Ladies or Gentlemen:

On February 1 I booked a trip to Las Vegas for Mr. and Mrs. Richard Schmidt of Macon, GA. As you advertised, the reservations specified a five-day stay at the Flamingo Hotel, from March 26 through March 31, 19—.

Mr. and Mrs. Schmidt have just returned from their trip and are quite disturbed. When they arrived at the Flamingo Hotel on the morning of March 26, they were told that there were no reservations in their name. The Flamingo Hotel was booked due to a convention, and the only hotel that had any vacancies was the Heartbreak Hotel. They would not have objected to staying at the Heartbreak Hotel, but it is in no way comparable to what they were expecting. My clients are requesting the return of the $250 they paid for their stay at the Heartbreak Hotel.

Please call me immediately so that we can arrange for an amicable settlement of this matter.

Sincerely,

Jean Silva, Manager

cc: Mr. and Mrs. Richard Schmidt

2 Anthony Street
Fountain Valley, CA 92608
March 3, 19—

Ms. Katherine E. Blythe
Penny Savings Bank
56 North Main Street
Fountain Valley, CA 92708

Dear Ms. Blythe:

Recently, I had the following problem with your bank. I deposited a check for $5,000 in the ATM on the morning of February 23. On that same day, you returned a check in the amount of $2,000, payable to the Sanders Trust Company, marked "insufficient funds." My bank statement indicates that the $5,000 deposit was made on February 24. That is not true. Please check your records again.

As a result of this error, I was charged $10 for the returned check and have suffered embarrassment with the Sanders Trust Company. I believe you should:

- Refund me the $10 I was charged for insufficient funds.

- Send a letter to the Sanders Trust Company [address] explaining that my account was not overdrawn—that it was a bank error.

- Write a letter of apology to me for my embarrassment and expense.

I await your comments. Thank you.

Very truly yours,

Sheila Fusco

ADJUSTMENTS

A prompt response is important in any situation, but it is essential when responding to a claim because it can help defuse a potentially unpleasant situation. Even if the claim must be studied before an answer can be given, let the customer know that his/her claim is being addressed. This can also be an opportunity to request additional information.

> Thank you for your letter of February 23 calling our attention to [issue]. I am investigating the situation and hope to have an answer for you within the next two weeks.

> In the meantime, would you please send me a copy of the bill of sale? This will give me the additional information I need to process this claim quickly.

Granting an Adjustment

This is generally a "good news letter" and is not very difficult to write. The following suggestions will be helpful:

1. *Acknowledge the claim and tell the reader the adjustment is being granted.* Never give the impression that you are making any special concessions, even if you are.

> It is easy to understand your frame of mind, [name], please accept my apology. To make amends, we are . . .

> As your letter of December 12 pointed out, Invoice #234 was indeed in error. The discount of 15% does apply to your latest purchase, and a revised invoice will be sent to you shortly. Please excuse the mistake, and we thank you for calling this to our attention.

2. *Stress the effort the company is making to prevent a recurrence of this event.* Accept the blame gracefully, and do not denounce an employee.

> As you can imagine, we are grateful that you suffered no injuries, and we wish to extend our apologies for this unpleasant experience. We are taking additional precautions to make certain that this does not happen again.

3. *End the letter on a positive note that will lead to future dealings.* Do not reiterate the incident that necessitated the adjustment. And do not overlook the possibility of promoting future sales.

> I am pleased to send you a $50 gift certificate towards the purchase of any merchandise in our catalog.

> When you need ski equipment, you will find everything from ski jackets to skis and bindings. You can continue to rely on our motto: "Satisfaction or your money back."

Situation: On August 12, you received an irate letter from Ms. Barbara Norman, a long-standing customer. She stated that the door is no longer open to your salesman, Vic Torian. Apparently, Mr. Torian has been pushy and rude and has presented a series of ridiculous schemes. Ms. Norman concluded with: "We no longer want [your product] or any further contact." Your response might be:

August 12, 19—

Ms. Barbara Norman
Berringer & Sons
456 Smith Street
Skokie, IL 60076

Dear Ms. Norman:

I am very sorry to learn of the problem you have had with our salesman, Vic Torian. All our salespeople attend a one-week training program because we expect them to be honest with and courteous to all our customers. Please accept my apology. We have taken corrective action regarding Mr. Torian, and you can be assured that he will not call on you again.

Ms. Norman, your business is important to us, and we are anxious to continue the long-standing relationship we have enjoyed for many years. I will call you personally next week to see how we may continue to offer you the fine service you have received over the last several years.

Sincerely,

William Marblehead

Situation: You received a letter from an irate customer whose order for a five-pound box of chocolate arrived in damaged condition.

SWEET SAVAGE CHOCOLATE
11 Sweet Treat Trail, Greenwich, CT 06836
(203) 661-6750

October 12, 19—

Mr. James F. Auger
2 Diana Place
Worcester, MA 01615

Dear Mr. Auger:

Thank you for taking the time to write us as you did on October 1. We know it must have been a disappointment to have received the box of chocolate in damaged condition. Our guess is that the damage occurred in transit. You do not need to do anything about the parcel post claim; we will take care of that here.

We mailed a new five-pound box to you today and trust that this one will arrive safely. We are proud of Sweet Savage Chocolate's candies and want our customers to be completely satisfied. Thank you for bringing this matter to our attention.

Enjoy!

Sincerely,

Lotta Kallories
President

Denying an Adjustment

Sometimes the customer is wrong and you cannot grant an adjustment. It is not always easy to write a letter of this nature and keep the customer's goodwill, but you must try. The following suggestions will be helpful:

1. *Start with a buffer that acknowledges the customer's point of view.* Show that you understand the problem and are trying to be fair.

   Thank you for relating the story of the delayed delivery of the luggage you purchased for your daughter. We are sorry that the delay caused you both so much anxiety.

2. *Give the explanation before the decision.* Stress what can be done, if anything. Do not blame or argue. And avoid expressions such as *your complaint, your error, we refuse.*

   Our one-year guarantee is made to cover only defective parts and workmanship. We had one of our engineers inspect the computer, and she found that the floppy drive had been damaged. We are wondering if perhaps the computer had been dropped.

   At the present time, all my student teachers are working under very heavy loads. Asking them to participate in a study, no matter how worthwhile, would be unfair to them. I compliment you on the topic you chose . . .

3. *Be courteous, even if the customer wasn't.* Otherwise you lose your self-respect and the customer.

4. *Try to end on a friendly note.* This is especially important because the customer thinks he/she is right.

Situation: You have just received a letter from Mr. Arthur Sharfin, President of Roy-Paul Co. Mr. Sharfin is quite upset because the invitations he ordered to celebrate the retirement of the company's CEO were not delivered on time. This forced him to invite his guests to the retirement dinner via Mailgrams. Mr. Sharfin would like to meet with you to reach an amicable settlement of this claim. He wants a full refund. Your response might be:

PRESTO PRINTING
300 Virginia Avenue, Minneapolis, MN 55438
(612) 245-5667

June 20, 19—

Mr. Arthur Sharfin
Roy-Paul Co.
234 Hampshire Avenue
Minneapolis, MN 55438

Dear Mr. Adler:

Your certified letter has just been handed to me. I know how important these invitations were to you and want you to be assured that our company did everything in its power to deliver them on time.

I am wondering if you are aware of the circumstances that led to the ten-day delay. Mr. Green, your Director of Advertising, held the dummy for two weeks before returning it; that initially put us behind schedule. The dummy was approved with the date of the celebration being the 15th of June, not the 16th. (We had no way of knowing that the 15th was incorrect.) We scheduled an overtime shift and met your deadline. After the invitations were delivered, Mr. Green noticed that the date was incorrect. He asked that the invitations be reprinted. Due to other scheduling crunches, we were unable to meet your deadline.

I will be out of town for the next week and will call you when I return so that we can arrange a mutually convenient time to discuss this matter. Once again, I am sorry that you were unable to use the invitations, but I believe once we have an opportunity to review all the details, you will see that we were not responsible for the delay.

I look forward to discussing this with you in person.

Sincerely,

Domenico P. Lombardi, President

Situation: An irate customer just dropped by the Customer Service Department with a nine-year-old lawn mower that is no longer working. He had a five-year warranty on the mower and is now demanding that it be fixed free of charge. You must tactfully refuse. Your response might be:

September 16, 19—

Mr. Charles E. Stoneham
3 Allegro Road
Cleveland, OH 44197-8066

Dear Mr. Stoneham:

You are right to expect top-quality merchandise from [store]. We have always prided ourselves on giving our customers the best merchandise for the best prices, and we stand behind everything we sell.

Thank you for bringing the lawn mower back to our store. After many hours of testing, our service manager determined that the mower's [specific parts] need to be replaced. It appears as if the lawn mower has not been maintained according to the instructions that accompanied it. The total repairs would cost $190. Would you like us to repair it?

Since the lawn mower is nine years old, you might consider replacing it. Please look for our flyer in the mail next week. It will be advertising some "early bird" spring specials which you might want to consider. With the proper care and maintenance, we are certain that a new lawn mower will give you longer service than the old one did.

Sincerely,

Karen Doherty
Customer Service Manager

Situation: You just received a letter from Leslie Atchinson, and you are not sure if Leslie is a male or female. Leslie is complaining about a hairpiece he/she purchased and wants his/her money returned. Federal law does not allow for the return of hairpieces.

August 29, 19—

Leslie Atchinson
115 Northeast Cutoff
Riverton, NJ 08077

Dear Leslie Atchinson:

Thank you for your letter of August 21 requesting that you return a hairpiece you recently purchased.

Generally, we accept returns of all merchandise that is in reasonable condition and is in compliance with state laws. Hairpieces, however, like underwear and bathing suits, fall under Federal health regulations and cannot be accepted for resale.

Please visit our local store [name and address] and, for a nominal fee, Mr. Wong, the store manager, will adjust your hairpiece to fit properly.

This will help you to have a hairpiece you will be proud to wear.

Very truly yours,

John R. Graf, Vice President

CLAIM

Dear Ms. Macaluso:

Re: Invoice No. 280DD-4

I did not appreciate the curt letter I received from your Credit Department yesterday regarding the above invoice, a copy of which is attached. I've been disputing these charges for two months. After having dealt with you for many years, I deserve better treatment.

Your competitors will be happy to honor my credit, and I will transfer my future business elsewhere.

Regretfully,

Lee Kirkwood

ADJUSTMENT

Dear Mr. Kirkwood:

Re: Invoice No. 280DD-4

You are absolutely right and you have my sincere apology. I personally checked into why you received the letter in question and acknowledge that the computer operator sent you the wrong letter.

Form letters such as the one you received are reserved for customers who have ignored invoices for more than four months. I have taken the liberty of straightening out the questions you had about the invoice in question and am pleased to tell you that your current balance is only $150.

Please accept my apologies for a letter that was completely undeserved. We look forward to continuing the long-standing relationship we have enjoyed over the years.

Sincerely,

Lisa Macaluso
Credit Manager

CLAIM

Dear Sir or Madam:

Re: Invoice No. 234AB

I recently purchased from your catalog OEM Toner Cartridge No. 123 for $74.99, which was advertised to be 20 percent below the normal price. I received the toner cartridge two days later and felt completely satisfied with my purchase.

While looking through the Sunday edition of THE BOSTON GLOBE yesterday, I noticed the same toner cartridge selling for $64.99 at Global Computer Outlet.

You say you won't be undersold on any merchandise. If that's true, I'd appreciate a refund of $10. Enclosed is a copy of Global's advertisement together with a photostatic copy of my invoice. Thank you.

Sincerely,

Skip Simmons

MAKING THE ADJUSTMENT

Dear Mr. Simmons:

We pride ourselves on our policy not to be undersold. Our customers must be completely satisfied with any merchandise they purchase from us, both for quality and price.

It is, therefore, with great pleasure that we send you the enclosed check in the amount of $10. Thank you for your continued support and patronage.

Sincerely,

John Rohner
General Manager

DENYING THE ADJUSTMENT

Dear Mr. Simmons:

We pride ourselves on our policy not to be undersold. Our customers must be completely satisfied with any merchandise they purchase from us, both for quality and price.

When I looked closely at the advertisement you sent from Global Computer Outlet, I noticed that the toner cartridge you refer to was for the Unit I printer, not the Unit II that you ordered. It was quite easy to see why the two would have been confused.

We do appreciate your bringing this matter to our attention and thank you for your continued support and patronage.

Sincerely,

John Rohner
General Manager

CHAPTER SIX

SALES AND PROMOTIONS

QUALITY—there simply is no substitute!

Don't miss this $$-making opportunity!

Give your children the head start they deserve!

WE MUST MOVE OUR INVENTORY

Crème de la crème

You owe it to yourself to . . .

Join the handful of people who . . .

CLAIM YOUR FREE . . .

America's foremost . . .

Prepare yourself for . . .

A sales letter is a written sales call. When you make a sales call, however, you already have gotten the prospect's attention. When you are sending a sales letter, you first need to get the prospect's attention. Sales and promotion letters have been and continue to be an effective selling tool. Letters are certainly less costly than media coverage and can be targeted to a specific audience.

Many people regard sales and promotion letters as junk mail and place such letters in the "circular file" unread. A five percent response rate is considered positive, so consider mass mailings and play the numbers.

PRINCIPLES OF A GOOD SALES AND PROMOTION LETTER

- *Learn all you can about your products and services.* What can they do? What can they not do? What are the advantages and disadvantages? What is the main appeal?

- *Know your customer base.* Learn all you can about them. Who are they? What are their needs? What are their "hot" buttons?

- *Understand the principles of good selling.* What motivates people? What gets them to respond?

PLANNING YOUR LETTER-WRITING CAMPAIGN

1. *Prepare a list of prospects.* Target this list to a specific group that has the common characteristics of your desired audience. (There are companies that specialize in selling lists.) For example, if you are promoting a sailing magazine, you must know that your prospects are sailors.

2. *Analyze the prospects.* Take into account sex, age, occupation, geographic location, financial situation, etc. For example, you would not try to sell lawn mowers to city apartment dwellers.

3. *Evaluate the products or services from the prospects' points of view.* What features should be emphasized? What makes the products or services most attractive to this particular group of prospects?

4. *Decide on the main selling point.* That could be appearance, durability, cost, convenience, comfort, education, etc.

5. *Plan the letter.* A standard formula for any sales or promotion letter is **AIDA.**

get the reader's	**A**ttention
pique the reader's	**I**nterest
create the	**D**esire
then call for	**A**ction

6. *Study the market and plan your mailing.* Timeliness is a key ingredient. For example, if your letter is promoting a special Christmas offer, it is important to know that heavy Christmas shopping starts the day after Thanksgiving.

Getting the Reader's Attention

Use an attention getter that captures the heart of the matter. This should address a need, an interest, or desire.

- *Start with an interesting or catchy phrase on the envelope.* If you want the prospect to read your "pitch," he/she must first open the envelope.

  VALUABLE DOCUMENT ENCLOSED
  $$-MAKING OPPORTUNITY
  DOUBLE YOUR SAVINGS
  STARTLING NEWS ABOUT . . .

  (I recently saw a very played-down envelope [similar to the one below] that caught my attention. It had the return address typed in the upper-left corner. Although I did not recognize the name, I opened the letter immediately because it looked like something personal. Whatever works!)

James G. Crowther
454 Main Street
Hudson, MA 01749

Ms. Eleanor Diozzi
55 Broadway
Cambridge, MA 02142

- *Arrange the first sentence as a headline.* It can be blocked, in color, in all caps, in a different font style, etc.

RIGHT NOW I'M INVITING YOU TO . . .

**Have you ever imagined
what it would be like
to . . .**

If [product] is your passion, then you'll appreciate . . .

- *Attach a simple object such as a button, a coin, etc.*

    This small bag of sand is just our way of reminding you that it's been a long time since we've had the pleasure of your company at the Sandy Beach Hotel.

    ___

    We've taken the liberty of permanently encasing in Plasticine your recent engagement announcement that appeared in THE WASHINGTON POST. As you can see, Plasticine is . . .

(Someone I know recently sent a resume to the Velcro company. She used a piece of Velcro to attach pages one and two. What a creative idea!)

- *Use a thought-provoking question or quotation.*

    Could you use additional income?

    ___

    Have you ever stayed awake at night thinking about . . .

    ___

    "Don't wait for your ship to come in—swim out to it."

    ___

    As a documentation specialist, you are undoubtedly spending a great deal of time focused on the development of others. When is the last time you took a couple of days to focus on YOUR professional development?

- *Start with an anecdote, a fable, or a parable.*

    The door closed slowly as Jon entered the President's office and sank into the dark leather chair in the far corner. Jon had been there many times but knew by the tone of the President's telephone conversation that she'd had another of her "brainstorms."

Holding the Reader's Interest and Creating a Desire

You captured the reader's attention. Now you must hold his/her interest and create a desire.

- *Plan the message around the reader—use the YOU approach.* Bring the reader into the picture by explaining how the products or services can be of direct benefit. Even though the reader might not be familiar with what you are promoting, he/she is interested in "self."

- *Keep the message, brief, interesting, and informative.* A letter that drags will wind up in the "circular file." The language and style should be easy to understand and relate to the reader's own situation. (Later in this chapter there will be a discussion about "Finding the Right Words.")

- *Be certain your information is accurate and honest.* You may fool people once, but you will not fool them twice. And most companies rely on repeat business.

- *Do not apply high-pressure and do not knock competitive products.* Do not try to force the reader to buy; people do not like to feel manipulated. If a product or service is good and well packaged, it will sell itself.

  If you're a newcomer to the [specific] industry, there's no faster way to learn the ABCs of the technology. If you're a seasoned professional, there's no better way to advance your skill and knowledge.

- *Introduce price at the best psychological moment.* If your key selling point is the price, introduce it early in the letter. If you think the price might seem high, focus first on the advantages.

Calling for Action

Always conclude by telling the reader what you expect him/her to do. You may want the reader to fill out an order blank, to call, to come to a seminar, etc.

  Remember, this offer is for one week only—and the sooner you respond the better. Once your order is in, you can be guaranteed continued service.

  Join the best of the imaging professionals—some 35,000 of them—for this once-a-year event. There is nothing like it in the world. Mail your registration form today.

  All you need to do is sign your name at the bottom of this letter and fax it to me. Your additional coverage will be effective immediately.

  Let us know when our sales representative may contact you. Just fill out the enclosed card and place it in the postage-paid envelope.

FINDING THE RIGHT WORDS

The following are some phrases that may be helpful in different situations:

Appeal for Contributions	Together we can . . . Whatever you send will mean so much. With your help, we'll be able to . . . You'll be able to say with great pride, "I've made a difference!"
Appeal to Senses	a pleasure to behold a rushing brook emerging from their long winter dormancy the wind in the trees
Authenticity	has withstood the test of time . . . often imitated but never equaled the original . . . There's simply no substitute for the real thing!
Classic	a nostalgic glimpse of . . . In the rich tradition of . . . . . . lets you relive . . . the glory of . . . endures the test of time.
Company Image	A commitment to excellence. Here are just a few of our clients: our total commitment We had the foresight to . . .
Convenient	eliminates the need for . . . located in the heart of . . . Now you can order direct. You'll never again have to . . .
Decision Time	Don't take our word for it. Experience it yourself. *You* decide. You have absolutely nothing to lose. You'll just have to experience it for yourself.
Experienced	Listen to what the experts say! We beat the competition hands down. We have vision. We're thoroughly familiar with . . .

Flattery	discriminating people . . . men and women of distinction You have been highly recommended by . . . Your . . . set(s) you apart from the general public.
Help	. . . guides you every step of the way Our job is to make your job easier. You can turn to us with confidence. Your . . . will receive our top priority.
Money Saving	A fraction of its original cost. Designer quality at affordable prices. Finally, a . . . you can afford. Why pay more for . . .
Salutations	Dear Customer: Dear Patron of the Arts: Greetings! Welcome to . . .
Satisfaction	Sit back and enjoy . . . . . . to your heart's content. Try a little self-indulgence. your passport to . . .
Status	among the most exclusive Until now only a select few have . . . where today's movers and shakers gather You'll be a member of an elite group.
Superior	a sterling example of . . . America's leading . . . our unparalleled reputation . . . There's just no substitute for the best.
Transitions	Before I say any more . . . For these and other reasons . . . Now, for the first time . . . With your permission, I'd like to . . .
Unusual	uniquely suited to . . . unprecedented You can leave the mainstream behind. You can search far and wide and still never find . . .

COMPILING A MAILING LIST

Mailing lists can help you reach a target audience. You can purchase mailing lists or solicit names from satisfied customers/clients. A letter soliciting names might read as follows:

Dear

If you've been satisfied with our [product/service], won't you please give us the names and addresses of a few [business associates/friends] who might also enjoy our [product/service].

We'll send them, without any obligation, some [literature, etc.].

Name _____
Street Address _____
City _____ State _____ ZIP _____
Telephone Number _____

Name _____
Street Address _____
City _____ State _____ ZIP _____
Telephone Number _____

Name _____
Street Address _____
City _____ State _____ ZIP _____
Telephone Number _____

Thank you for your continued support.

Sincerely,

Mailing List Sources

- City and state directories
- City and state licensing bureaus
- Clubs and professional organizations
- Commercial agencies that specialize in selling mailing lists

- Conventions and conferences
- Educational directories
- Mercantile directories
- Newspapers (columns or special articles)
- *Standard and Poor's Register of Corporations*
- *Thomas Register of American Manufacturers*
- Trade directories
- Trade publications

FOLLOW-UP TO VISITORS AT TRADE SHOW BOOTH

At trade shows, companies will often have depositories where people can leave business cards. Many companies will send a follow-up letter to everyone who leaves a card.

Dear

Thank you for visiting our booth at the recent [type] conference in [city]. We hope you enjoyed it as much as we did.

Many who visited our booth commented on the latest features of [product].

- [List of features you are promoting.]
-
-

Enclosed is a brochure which describes [product] in greater detail. If you are interested in learning more about [product], please call us toll free at [number] and ask for [name].

Sincerely,

Solicitation (Form Letter)

Dear

- [List typical problems the customer may have.]
-
-
-

If you can identify with one or more of these situations, let's get together to discuss how [company] can help you. [Give some brief information about your company's accomplishments in dealing with these issues.]

I will call you early next week to set up a mutually convenient time for us to get together.

Sincerely,

HELPFUL HINT

Save the sales and promotion letters you receive. You would be surprised at how many ideas they contain that might be helpful in planning yours. The following are some I have been accumulating.

Advertising Age

965 East Jefferson
Detroit, Michigan 48207

January 29, 19—

Mr. John Bennington
Vice-President Marketing
Ford Motor Company
1921 Fairlane Drive
Dearborn, MI 48107

"We need someone with vision, creativity, and great marketing instincts... someone like John Bennington."

Cartoon courtesy of *Advertising Age.*

Dear Mr. Bennington:

The Publisher of *Advertising Age* asked me to make a very special subscription offer to a small, select group of advertising and marketing professionals. Your name was submitted to me as one who qualifies.

So . . . here it is—a private invitation to subscribe to *Advertising Age* at the best discount I can offer—a savings of $19 off the regular subscription price. And, if you send in your subscription order by March 12, 19—, you will also receive an 8 X 10, suitable-for-framing gallery print of the cartoon above, personalized with your name.

This limited edition cartoon by famous *New Yorker* cartoonist Leo Cullum will be personalized with your name, and mailed to you absolutely free and with our compliments.

This opportunity to subscribe to *Advertising Age* at such a low rate is being offered to you, Mr. Bennington, because we are sure that you will benefit from the advertising, marketing, and media news and analysis which *Advertising Age* provides each week.

You see, just because you're reading this letter we know this much about you—in one way or another you're in the business of making products or services move. And that you're a busy man. Long hours. Short deadlines. High expectations. And intense commitment. Few people realize what you go through every day. And only a couple of business publications even come close to meeting your unique information requirements.

That's because—to deliver the knowledge you need—a publication would have to live inside your world. Understand your job. And feel the pulse of every segment of the industry that impacts yours.

over please...

That's *Advertising Age*—and that has been our only mission for over 60 years.

In each weekly issue, *Ad Age* delivers news, features, and analysis on every aspect of the marketing process. Nothing important is skipped. Market research and testing. New product development and packaging. Ad budgets, media strategy, media buying. Sales Promotion. Direct Marketing. International marketing news. Accounts up for grabs. The key players—people making the key decisions. People on the way up—people on the way out. Client news, brand news, agency news, media news.

You'll be among the first to discover the closely guarded marketing strategies of the world's leading companies and agencies. Then you'll see the competitors develop their counter-strategy. It all unfolds in the pages of *Ad Age* every week.

You'll get the latest, hottest advertising and marketing news from around the world, and in your own backyard. You may even get your next job from "The Advertising Marketplace," the most widely read classified section in the entire world of advertising.

You'll be inspired by the international creative brilliance which *Advertising Age* covers like no one else. You'll see the latest creative trends and market-shaking promotions. You'll see what's working . . . and who's creating it.

Everything essential is covered—and covered intelligently. In fact, we guarantee that you'll never be at a loss for the most current news, information, and knowledge in the business. If you're ever not 100% satisfied, just let us know. We'll stop your subscription, and you'll get a full refund—no questions asked.

You are invited to subscribe to *Advertising Age* at this time at a special private-offer subscription rate. Your rate—just $67 for an entire 51-issue year—is a full $19 off the regular subscription price.

To activate your subscription please complete the enclosed Acceptance Certificate and mail it in today in the postage-paid envelope provided. That's all you need to do. I'll make sure that your own personal copy of *Ad Age* shows up on your desk every week.

But please, make sure you reply today. This is a special private offer. As a result, we must request that your Acceptance Certificate be mailed no later than March 12, 19—.

Sincerely,

Dave Kelley

Dave Kelley
Subscription Manager

"We need someone with vision, creativity, and great marketing instincts... someone like John Bennington."

Mr. John Bennington
Vice-President Marketing
Ford Motor Company
1921 Fairlane Drive
Dearborn, MI 48107

Cartoon courtesy of *Advertising Age*

acucobol **inc**

April 26, 19–

Downsizing!   Rightsizing!   Smartsizing!

No matter what you call it, there's a revolution going on in organizations like yours. Stuck with hundreds of older computers that are gobbling up dollars and slowing user service to a crawl, many agencies are taking drastic steps to cut costs and improve performance.

But moving from a larger platform to a smaller, more powerful one is not as simple as the trade press would have you believe. Rumor and horror stories abound. Do you rewrite using a fourth generation language? What about your investment in legacy COBOL code? How do you downsize without making critical errors? Can't anyone give you a straight answer?

In a word—YES! You'll get answers to these and many other questions in a high-energy, half-a-day seminar appropriately entitled *"The Downsize, Rightsize, Smartsize Information Systems Seminar."* Our presenter is Bill Fried, high tech author, international downsizing expert and Executive Vice President of Acucobol, Inc. He's smart, he's entertaining, and, most importantly, he's been there.

Bill will give you the straight facts, without the hype, on how to downsize your existing COBOL application risk free. You'll learn how Fortune 500 companies like **Westinghouse** and **Leggett & Platt** are already using this proven method to save millions of dollars, while at the same time transforming their organizations into highly efficient user-driven powerhouses.

Don't miss this informative, free morning seminar. See the enclosed seminar schedule for dates and locations.

Very truly yours,

Cameron Jenkins
Vice President

7950 Silverton Avenue

Suite 201

San Diego, CA 92126

Phone 619.689.7220
Fax 619.566.3071
1.800.262.6585

COMPUTER
LANGUAGE
PRODUCTIVITY
AWARD

Dear Member:

A couple of weeks ago, I spent an evening with three of my neighbors. During the evening, I described our *AAA Guaranteed Life* policy to them. I wanted to get their reactions.

"I'm impressed," said one neighbor. "Neither my insurance at work nor my personal insurance builds cash values for me. I can't borrow on them—and I don't get a penny if I cancel."

Another neighbor said, "I like the feature that a member never has to pay more than he paid the first year—no matter how many years he is insured. With one of my policies, I pay more each five years. And with another policy, the amount of my insurance keeps going down every year I have the policy."

The third neighbor remarked, "What I like about the policy is that it's so easy to buy. Just send in the application by mail. And no medical examination. And you're guaranteed the application will be accepted—even if the member has a health problem. Great!"

Those comments were music to my ears. You see, we worked hard to put many fine features into this *AAA Guaranteed Life* policy. And the reason your acceptance is guaranteed is simply because the death benefit is reduced in the first two years you own your plan. You'll read about this feature and all the others in Mr. Atkins' letter—and throughout this mailing.

Here's one small example. Because you and our other members are all motorists, we made this policy even more valuable by having it pay *double* if an auto accident takes the member's life.

Please take a moment now to get acquainted with *AAA Guaranteed Life*'s valuable features.

Sincerely yours,

Timothy Montgomery
President

Dear Patient:

I'd like to share with you some things that are going on in our practice and in dentistry in general. As you know, these are difficult economic times. I've personally shared experiences with many patients as well as with doctors and dentists. To help combat the economic impact on my patients, I've been holding my fees in check since 1989 and will continue to do so. I feel that medical and dental fees in this country are way out of line, and each of us must do our share.

Many of you have asked about AIDS or other infectious diseases and how I deal with this in my dental office. Let me assure you that I follow all the guidelines of the American Dental Association, the Federal Drug Administration, and the Occupational Safety and Health Administration. All of our instruments are either steam-heat autoclaved or are disposable. We also follow universal precautions by wearing gloves and face masks. We have been taking these precautions for many years in order to provide you with the highest standards of care.

Many of you have also asked, "Doctor, are you accepting new patients?" The answer is, "Yes, yes, yes." I can only maintain the high level of patient care by having a constant source of new patients, and *I very much welcome your referrals.*

In the future, I will be producing a short newsletter about current ideas in dentistry and other matters that affect our patients. If you have any thoughts or ideas that you'd like included, I'd enjoy receiving them.

Cordially,

Donald I. Rothenberg, D.M.D.

DONALD I. ROTHENBERG, D.M.D. • 11 ANGENICA TERRACE • MARBLEHEAD • MA 01945 • (617) 639-2585

THE PRACTICE OF GENERAL AND IMPLANT DENTISTRY

Engineering Recruiting Specialists

1500 West Park Drive   Westborough Office Park   Westborough, Massachusetts 01581   508/366-2600   Fax 508/898-0115

May 10, 19—

Mr. Robert N. Donelson
Allegro MicroSystems, Inc.
115 Northeast Causeway
Worcester, MA 01615

Source Engineering is engaged in a search for a semiconductor process engineer for a client in Massachusetts. To qualify, the candidate must have a total 5+ years' experience which should include at least three of the following areas:

- Photo Resist and Etch
- Diffusion
- Thin Film
- Epitaxial Growth and CVD

If you know someone who may qualify, call me at (508) 366-2600. You may also contact me by FAX (508) 898-0115 or by mail.

Please complete the following if you can lead me to a colleague who is qualified.

CANDIDATE'S NAME _____
TITLE _____
ADDRESS _____
CITY _____
STATE _____ ZIP _____
TELEPHONE: HOME _____ WORK _____

All the Best,

Michael R. Neece
SOURCE ENGINEERING

Would you toss away money that was given to you absolutely free—with no strings attached?

You might say "no," but that's what thousands of families do each year. We're sure you won't make the same mistake. You and your family have been selected from many others to enjoy this once-in-a lifetime opportunity. You're invited to participate in a $1,000 cash drawing . . . enjoy a sumptuous lunch . . . and spend an afternoon at one of the nation's most prestigious resorts.

Let me explain. *Seaside Delights* is a community developer who's interested in letting families know about the time-sharing opportunities that await you in Virginia Beach. All you need to do is fill out the attached response card and circle which of the four Saturday afternoons you'd like to share with us. You'll join us for a brief orientation and seaside buffet luncheon. You'll have the opportunity to spend the day swimming, playing volleyball, and enjoying a host of other activities.

This is a wonderful opportunity, not a gimmick! And there are no strings attached. If you disregard this invitation, you'll be throwing away cash. Make yours one of the lucky families to experience paradise, just a short distance from home.

Sincerely,

Sandy Sheldon

SEASIDE DELIGHTS
One Sandy Beach Drive
Virginia Beach, VA 00000

SEASIDE DELIGHTS
One Sandy Beach Drive
Virginia Beach, VA 00000

Would you toss away money absolutely free
that was given to you
—with no strings attached?

C◇RATS

May 1, 19—

Dear Valued Customer:

This is our fifth year in business, and we are pleased to announce that we've grown to where it has become necessary to move to larger quarters. As of May 15, our new location will be:

One Essex Street
Essex Building
Falls Church, VA 22042
(703) 875-5100

The Essex Building is just across the street from the Falls Church Savings and Loan Association. We'll occupy the entire third floor of the Essex Building. There is ample free parking in back of the building, and the Essex Building is also accessible via mass transportation.

On behalf of everyone at CARATS, we want to thank you for your continued support which has made this wonderful move possible. Please accept our invitation to let us welcome you personally to our new quarters. To help you celebrate our success, we're offering a 10% discount to the first 25 customers who make a purchase of $500 or more. As always, we're anxious to serve you.

Cordially,

Pearl Ruby
General Manager

One Essex Street, Essex Building, Falls Church, VA 22042
(703) 875-5100

CHAPTER SEVEN

INQUIRIES, REQUESTS, AND RESPONSES

> *Por favor . . . Gracias*
>
> *Bitteschön . . . Dankeschön*
>
> *S'il vous plait . . . Merci*

We each receive and ask many questions throughout the course of a day. Some questions get the desired results; others do not. Have you ever wondered why?

INQUIRIES AND REQUESTS

In any language, *please* and *thank you* go a long way. Always appreciate the service the receiver is being asked to perform. If your letter has a warm and courteous tone, the receiver will *want* to help you. Remember to include your name, address, and phone number so the receiver will be able to respond.

Solicited Inquiries and Requests

When your request is expected, you will not need to write volumes leading to the request. Get to the point quickly by stating exactly what you are asking. Also, include the name of your source.

> Please send me answers to the following questions about the skis that are advertised on page 5 of SKI ADVENTURES magazine:

Unsolicited Inquiries and Requests

When your request is unsolicited, you need to give the receiver all the background information he or she will need to respond: How? Why? When? Where? or Who?

- *Begin with your question and why you are asking.*

  > Would it be convenient for me to stop by your office next Monday to demonstrate our new EDI software?

- *Ask only for the necessary information.*

- *Make your inquiries easy to answer.* When appropriate, include a questionnaire; a survey; a self-addressed, stamped envelope; a brochure, etc.

  > Won't you do your best to help us? Contributions are so badly needed. The enclosed self-addressed envelope will make it easy to put your check in the mail today.

- *Give a time by which you must have your reply.*

  > Please confirm my reservations immediately because I will be out of the office after September 3.

- *Point out the benefits the respondent might receive, if any.*

  > If you'd like to see my new designs, I'll be happy to stop by your office early next week. Just name the time and day which would be most convenient. I feel certain that you will be excited by the new line I'm proposing. This could have you up and running in time for the Spring showing.

- *Make it clear whether or not (and how) you expect to pay, if appropriate.*

  > If you would notify me when the purchase has been made and invoice me for your brokerage fees, I would appreciate it very much.

- *Leave an opening for a refusal if it is a delicate situation.*

  Can we have the 5,000 announcements by Friday of next week? I realize that we are asking the impossible. We would be willing to pay overtime charges if need be.

- *Promise respect for confidentiality if that might be an issue.*

  We shall be grateful for your opinions and shall regard them as confidential.

- *Close with your appreciation.* This can be a possible action, or looking forward to the next meeting.

  From the bottom of our hearts, we thank you for your generosity.

PATRIOTIC ACTION GROUP
5 Sheldon Drive, Delmont, PA 15626
(412) 468-1357

Dear Neighbor:

Please help your party now—when your help can really count.

We ask for your vote in support of Corinne Reppucci, who is a candidate for the House of Representatives from the state of Pennsylvania. Ms. Reppucci has proposed a program that will restore good government to the state of Pennsylvania and to America. She has made many inroads in elevating our state's educational system and has been an advocate of health care reform—two issues so near and dear to the hearts of our community.

Please take a moment to look over the enclosed brochure. You will see that Ms. Reppucci has been an upstanding and respected member of our community for the past thirty years and will continue to win issues that are important.

Sincerely,

Jean Woods

Why
did you let this happen?
Your subscription to HEALTHWAY has expired.

Dear Subscriber:

You must have a reason for not renewing your subscription to HEALTHWAY. May we ask why? If we haven't lived up to your expectations, please let us know. We would really appreciate hearing from you.

Perhaps your budget is a bit tight these days. Whose isn't? At HEALTHWAY, we're making every effort to keep our subscription rates low (compared to other similar magazines) and still maintain the kind of look, style, and editorial commentary you've come to expect.

Perhaps you meant to renew but misplaced the renewal form. Don't waste another minute. Fill out the enclosed renewal. Or call us at the number below.

Our renewal subscription rate is $18.00 a year—just half that of the newsstand price. You can renew now, and we'll bill you later.

The next issue is on the press. Let us put your name right where it belongs—on your monthly copy of HEALTHWAY.

Cordially,

Andrea Elizabeth Roberts
Circulation Editor

HEALTHWAY
12 Circle Boulevard, Corvallis, OR 97330-1234 * 1-800-234-0970

[Follow-up to Subscription]

November 7, 19—

Ms. Dale Phelps
23 Roberts Road
Owasso, OK 47055

Dear Ms. Phelps:

Welcome! It's good news that you will be with us as a subscriber for the next year.

Your subscription to HEALTHWAY Magazine has been entered, and your first issue will be arriving shortly. We've sent along an invoice which shows the amount that is due. Please look it over and make sure we've entered your name and address correctly.

Also, let us know if there is anything we can do to help you enjoy and benefit from our magazine. Just say the word, and we'll do our best to take care of your request.

We are pleased to have you as a subscriber and will take pride in giving you the best possible subscription service.

Cordially,

Andrea Elizabeth Roberts
Circulation Editor

REAL ESTATE "R" US

30 Prescott Boulevard, Elk Grove Village, IL 60007
(708) 437-8906

June 2, 19—

Ms. Stephanie Ferrante
ReMAX Realty Co.
344 Main Street
New City, NY 10956

Dear Ms. Ferrante:

For many years, your handbook entitled MAKING THAT "REAL" SALE has helped me with many of my sales problems, especially in this difficult marketplace. I have found Chapter II, which deals with broker-client relationships, to be particularly thought provoking.

I am now preparing a real estate report that will be printed and distributed to salespeople throughout our organization. I would like to cite the self-analysis chart that appears on page 134. May I have permission to use the material? I will, of course, give credit to the source. Please sign the attached copyright release and return it to me in the self-addressed, stamped envelope.

I am grateful for the help your handbook has given me all these years and am certain that the self-analysis chart will be helpful to all our salespeople who are working toward their goals of increased sales.

Sincerely,

Ted E. Bear

RESPONSES

When you answer an inquiry you are in a wonderful position to build goodwill, stimulate confidence, or generate sales. YOU are the one who assumes the responsibility for pushing that sale towards completion or for smothering the flicker of interest. The following guidelines will be helpful to both types of inquiry replies—those granting or refusing the request.

- *Answer promptly*—the sooner the better. If you are unable to give the inquirer the information he or she has requested, answer promptly promising the information at whatever time it will be available.

  > I believe that our manager, Mr. Jim Edwards, may be better able to help with your design problems than I. Mr. Edwards will be out of town until the 15th of this month, and I know this matter will receive his immediate attention once he returns. If there is any help that I can give to you personally at another time, I would be happy to hear from you again.

- *Express appreciation for the inquiry.* This can be done either directly or by the tone of the letter.

  > We appreciate your request of January 3, which gives us the opportunity to share with you the information about the Marlborough Chamber of Commerce.

- *Answer clearly, courteously, and completely.*

- *Remember to say "thank you."*

  > We are so pleased that you thought of us for . . .
  > Thanks indeed for . . .
  > We are most happy to . . .

- *If you say you will enclose something or send it later, be certain you do!*

Granting the Request

Everyone enjoys hearing "Yes, we can . . ."; say so in the beginning of your letter. Then follow that good news with how and when. The following guidelines will be helpful:

- *Give complete and specific details.* Start with the information the customer is most anxious to have.

In response to your request about our flexi-plan insurance policy, I am pleased to enclose a brochure which outlines its many benefits and conveniences.

- *Hold the customer's interest by detailing favorable information.*

    The plan may be tailored to fit the needs of your organization with a choice of credit cards for as many individuals as you designate. Yet, you will receive one itemized monthly bill for the travel of all card holders under the account.

- *Inject a sales component into the letter, if appropriate.* This must be done tactfully and without pressure.

    Because of your apparent interest in camping, perhaps you would want to subscribe to our new publication, CAMP SAVVY. I've enclosed a sample magazine for you to review, which contains a handy order form for your convenience.

Refusing the Request

Requests are generally reasonable and are granted, but occasionally someone will make a request that is unreasonable, and you will have to say "No." It might seem difficult to say "No" and still maintain the customer's goodwill, but it can be done. The following guidelines show how to accomplish this:

- *Start with a friendly buffer paragraph.* Let the recipient know you do appreciate the request.

    Thank you for your recent letter which was directed to the attention of our treasurer. We gave your request careful consideration because we recognize what a worthwhile cause it is.

- *Tactfully tell the reader why you cannot say "Yes."* Avoid a negative refusal.

    Please understand that in a company such as ours—with more than 25 divisions—it's impossible to support every worthwhile cause. Instead, each year the corporation makes a generous donation to the United Way.

    Many groups throughout the country have enjoyed our video [title]. It has become our most popular film. Last April we had ten more copies made to make it available to more people, and we still cannot keep up with the demand.

It's unfortunate that we won't be able to hold [merchandise] for that length of time because of our limited storage space. To compensate for this, we would be more than happy to . . .

* *Close pleasantly with a look to the future.*

Why don't you check with us again in a month or so. We are always hearing of new opportunities.

Meanwhile, if we hear of any cancellations, we will surely . . .

We appreciate your interest and are glad to know that you provide such a service. Perhaps at some time in the future we will be able to take advantage of it.

September 16, 19——

Dear Bob,

For several months I have been expecting you to hold the annual Rotary Club banquet sometime in October, and I've been keeping my fingers crossed that I would be able to attend.

Unfortunately, however, October 9 is out of the question for me. I'll be in San Francisco for the entire week attending our company's annual sales kick-off.

My sincere thanks for your gracious invitation. I hope this year's banquet will be the best ever. Under your capable guidance, I'm sure it will.

Perhaps next year!

Cordially,
Steve

LONGFELLOW ASSOCIATES
200 Bronx Road, Dallas, TX 75231

(214) 754-2345

March 10, 19—

Ms. Alexandra Edwards
Volunteers of America
One Montreal Parkway
Las Vegas, NV 98119

Dear Ms. Edwards:

We would very much like to take advertising space in your souvenir program, for most of the people who ask us to advertise are our friends and members of our community.

In the course of a year, however, we receive thousands of requests from the many worthwhile organizations. Consequently, we have had to adopt a policy of saying "No, thank you" to everyone— treating all requests alike. While it would be much more pleasant to say "Yes," I'm certain you will understand.

We do appreciate your interest in Longfellow Associates and wish you success in your undertaking.

Cordially,

Frank N. Stein
Vice President

FNS/sl

[Accepting a Speaking Engagement]

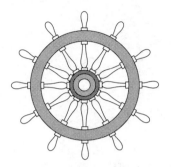

May 2, 19—

Mr. David Warburton, Public Relations
Sail-Away Yacht Club
3 Dearborne Lane
Annapolis, MD 21401

Dear Mr. Warburton:

It is my pleasure to accept your invitation to speak at the dinner meeting of the Sail-Away Yacht Club on July 8, 19—, at eight o'clock to tell about my experiences sailing across the Atlantic. After all those harrowing weeks at sea, there were times I thought it was unlikely that I should ever have the opportunity to relate my experiences to anyone. So I am especially grateful to you for providing such a sympathetic audience.

Yes, the Sunset Hotel would be a wonderful place for you to arrange my lodging. I will plan to drive to the hotel at about five, which will give me ample time to freshen up.

I also appreciate your proposing my name for membership in the prestigious Sail-Away Yacht Club, and I accept with pleasure.

Sincerely,

Betty Gau

[Declining a Speaking Engagement]

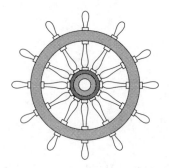

May 2, 19—

Mr. Dave Warburton, Public Relations
Sail-Away Yacht Club
3 Dearborne Lane
Annapolis, MD 21401

Dear Mr. Warburton:

Your invitation to speak at the dinner meeting of the Sail-Away
Yacht Club on July 8, 19—, at eight o'clock is one that I would very
much like to accept.

Unfortunately, I am committed to teach sailing classes during the
entire month of July. Would it be possible for me to speak to your
group later in the year? After all those harrowing weeks at sea,
there were times I thought it was unlikely that I should ever have
the opportunity to relate my experiences to anyone, and I would
certainly welcome the opportunity.

I also appreciate your proposing my name for membership in the
prestigious Sail-Away Yacht Club, and I accept with pleasure.

Sincerely,

Betty Gau

CHAPTER EIGHT

ORDERS AND ACKNOWLEDGMENTS

ORDERS

Dear Sir or Madam:

I've finally used up the scrap fabric I've been saving all these years stitching a quilt I've been making. I've now run out of fabric and need more yardage in order to finish the quilt. I particularly need black and white check to match the border I started.

I've checked with my local fabric store and they recommended that I contact you. Please send me scrap yardage of the black and white check. I don't have a copy of your current catalog, so I can't get the number of the fabric.

I'll gladly pay you for the fabric.

Very truly yours,

If you received a letter like the one above, you would either throw it out or pull your hair out.

THE FORMULA

In this fast-paced society of ours, mail order has become a popular means of shopping. In most instances, you will have an order blank or a number to call, but there may be instances when you will not. If you are ordering merchandise via a letter, follow these guidelines, using column format for the specifics of the order.

- *Start with a direct and definite request for merchandise*

  Please send me . . .
  I would like to order . . .

- *Source* (Specific catalog, flyer, etc.)

- *Complete description of merchandise* (Catalog number, color, grade, size, weight, model, or other special distinctions)

- *Quantity* (List quantity for each item or class of items, including dozen, gross, pounds, etc.)

- *Cost* (Unit cost, extension [cost × quantity], postage and insurance, applicable tax, total)

- *Method of payment* (Check, money order, or specific charge account information. Of course, you would never send cash through the mail.)

- *Mailing address* (If the mailing address differs from the address on the letterhead, be sure to include it. If letterhead is not used, be sure to include the shipping address.)

- *Method of shipment* (If you do not specify the method of shipment, your parcel will undoubtedly be mailed via parcel post or freight. If you need the order in a hurry, specify that you are willing to pay additional postage for one of the express services.)

Dear Sir or Madam:

Please send me the following merchandise as advertised on page 27 in the fall edition of your catalog:

Quantity	Catalog No.	Description	Unit Price	Total Price
10 yards	34-1A	black & white check	$3.98	$39.80
		Shipping and Handling		5.00
		Tax (6%)		2.69
		Total		$47.49

Enclosed is my check in the amount of $47.49. Please ship this via parcel post to my office. The address is 345 Center Street, Temple, CT 06103.

Very truly yours,

If you received a letter like the one above, you would be able to fill the order immediately.

ACKNOWLEDGING ORDERS

Regardless of the channel through which an order is placed, it should be acknowledged within two or three days. Some companies acknowledge orders routinely—doing so creates a closer personal relationship between the customer and the company—others do so only under special circumstances. A letter of acknowledgment should definitely be sent, if:

- the delivery will be delayed

- a substitute must be made

- you need more information

- an order can only be partially filled

- an order cannot be filled

Some companies that are particularly public-relations–minded often send acknowledgments to a customer who is ordering for the first time or is placing an exceptionally large order. You can use a simple acknowledgment card such as the one below.

Thank you for your order for
[merchandise].

Your order will be shipped on [date].

It's a pleasure to serve you and we
hope to have that privilege often.

————————— *Lorenz's* —————————

Delivery Will Be Delayed

When an order cannot be filled promptly, write to the customer immediately explaining the reason for the delay and when the order will arrive. A prompt and friendly acknowledgment can be more important than prompt delivery. A customer will understand a legitimate reason for a delay but will not understand long, silent waiting periods. Follow these suggestions:

- *Start with a positive, indirect approach.*

  Yes: Thank you for your order for [merchandise].

  No: We regret to inform you that . . .

- *Give the specific reason for the delay.* The customer must not think these delays are usual.

> *Out of Stock*

Yes: Because of the unusually hot weather we have been experiencing, the demand for air conditioners has been incredible.

No: We are temporarily out of stock.

> *More Information Is Needed*

Yes: We are grateful to you for your order sent to us on May 3. We are enclosing a reply card on which we would like you to state your color preference. Once we receive the card, we will process your order immediately.

No: Because you forgot to mention the color, we cannot process your order.

- *Express appreciation for the order and tell the customer when the order can be expected.*

We've called the manufacturer and have been assured that the unit will be shipped directly to you within the next ten days, perhaps sooner. We are truly sorry for any discomfort this has caused.

- *Close with some good points about the merchandise and your appreciation for the customer's business.*

This summer is forecasted to be the hottest on record in the last ten years, so we are sure you will get many months of pleasure and comfort from the air conditioner, which comes with a five-year warranty.

Again we are sorry for any inconvenience this has caused, and we thank you for shopping at Lorenz's.

Substitute Must Be Made

When you need to substitute one item for another—even if the substitution is minor—always notify the customer. Follow the suggestions above, adding the reason for the substitution.

Lorenz's   4 Mashlea Road, Monsey, NY 10952
(914) 352-7846

March 1, 19—

Ms. Ethel Sharfin
3 Ternure Avenue
Salem, MA 01970

Dear Ms. Sharfin:

Thank you for your recent order for ten reams of [identify the order].

Just this morning we were notified by the manufacturer that this paper stock has been discontinued. We have, however, located stock that is almost identical, and we are quite excited about it. It is called [identify the new merchandise] and we plan to carry it as part of our standard line.

The prices are comparable and we are certain you will be satisfied with its high quality. We have enclosed a sample and hope you will find that it meets your high standards. As soon as you give us the go-ahead, we will send the ten reams of [new merchandise] to you immediately.

We apologize for any delay this may have caused and assure you that we always do everything possible to offer you Lorenz's finest.

Sincerely,

Marilyn N. Harry
Sales Manager

CHAPTER NINE

PERSONAL BUSINESS (OR GOODWILL)

 Every business person will have occasion to write personal business letters. These letters can range from responses to good or bad news to exchanges between long-time friends and acquaintances. Each time you add a personal sentiment to a business letter, you turn it into a personal business letter that will create goodwill.

When you put a little of your heart into a letter, the effects go a long way. Take the opportunity to thank a staff member for a job well done . . . to express regrets to a staff member who has been let go . . . to express condolences to a staff member . . . to thank someone for a favor . . . to offer encouragement to a staff member who is experiencing difficult circumstances.

This chapter contains the following personal business letters:

- Favors
- Gifts
- Encouragement
- Congratulations
- Recommending Membership to an Organization or Club
- Thanking a Volunteer for a Major Project
- Congratulating an Employee for Years of Service
- Apology
- Commendations

CHARACTERISTICS OF A PERSONAL BUSINESS LETTER

A personal business letter can be typewritten, handwritten, or type-written with a handwritten notation. It should be:

- *Brief.* There is nothing wrong with a letter that is composed of one sentence or one paragraph.

  Dear Allie, I'm so very proud of you.

- *Thoughtful, honest, and prompt.*

  It was wonderful running into you at the seminar yesterday. I was particularly glad to hear that you joined the partnership of Ballock and Company. Perhaps . . .

  Let me take this opportunity to wish you and Susan a very happy and healthy New Year.

- *Persuasive without exaggerating.* It would be a great exaggeration to say, "I'll bet you a million bucks that . . ."

Letterhead or no letterhead?

Letterhead should be reserved for company business. Do not use letterhead for messages that are: controversial, for political or fund-raising purposes, for money-making activities disassociated with the company, or for purely personal matters.

What about the salutation?

When writing to a peer with whom you are comfortable, the first name (Dear Ed) is appropriate. When writing to a senior executive and you are uncertain but do not want to appear too formal, both names (Dear Ed Smith) are appropriate. If in doubt, the more formal last name (Dear Mr. Smith) is appropriate.

FAVORS

It is easier to request or decline a favor when you are not facing some-one. Therefore, "If in doubt, write it out."

Requesting a Favor

Open with a personal message, give the person the opportunity to refuse, and personalize the closing.

> It was delightful seeing you and Georgianna at the Sullivans' party last week. Those wonderful tans were certainly an indication that you're finally taking time to get away.
>
> I'd like to ask you a big favor and certainly understand that this is last-minute notice. [Detail all the information.]
>
> Again, I understand that this is the last minute, and you may already have prior commitments. In any event, please send my warmest regards to Georgianna.

Declining a Favor

Open with an expression of your inability, give a short explanation, close with hope of being of assistance in the future.

> It's tough refusing a favor to someone who's been so kind to me. However, I . . .
>
> I did take the liberty of calling Jonathan to see if he would be available, and he's going to be out of town. Perhaps you might want to give Gerald Graffo a call. You can probably reach him at . . .
>
> I hope that the next time you need me, I'll be "Johnny on the spot."

GIFTS

Gifts are part of our business culture and are often considered perks. A gift expresses "thank you," "I'm sorry," "congratulations," and a host of other sentiments. A gift can be a turkey for Thanksgiving, tickets to the theater or a ballgame, an expensive product, or a free trip. Whether you are giving or acknowledging a gift, a personalized note is always appropriate.

Sending a Gift

Today ABC Corporation will distribute $1 million in Performance Incentive Awards among employees in recognition of their contributions to our success in 19—. Without the individual efforts of each of you, we would be unable to provide the high-quality services to our customers. Thank you for your hard work and great accomplishments. Congratulations!

Please accept this gold pen as a token of our appreciation for your outstanding team efforts. Without your hard work and dedication, we would not be able to meet our corporate objectives and provide the high quality of service to our clients.

Acknowledging a Gift

When you laid the little gift on my desk two days before my birthday and said it was a "little remembrance," I must admit it was all I could do to wait until the day of my birthday to open it. Thank you so much for the wonderful book and for your usual good taste.

Dear Mel,

    I'd like to acknowledge the software you recently sent—it is first-rate. It was easy to install, easy to use, and performed exactly as we had hoped it would. I'm sure your company has a winner with this one.

    Thanks for allowing us to try your software because it did exactly what we needed it to do.

    Please feel free to use this letter as an endorsement.

               Sincerely,

               Rich

Acknowledging an Inappropriate Gift

Express your thanks in a very low-key manner.

It was a pleasant surprise to receive the nice gift from you. I appreciate the thought and send you and your family my best wishes.

Refusing a Gift

In many companies, it is against policy to accept a gift under any circumstances. If you are in the position of having to return or refuse a gift, great tact is required.

> It is so kind of you to remember me during this Christmas holiday. Your gift is so generous and so thoughtful. However, it is against company policy to accept gifts of any sort; therefore, I must return it. I know how much thought went into selecting [gift] and I greatly appreciate it.
>
> I want to wish you a very wonderful holiday and success for the new year.

ENCOURAGEMENT

There is nothing more comforting to people in distress than the care and concern of others. A personal note expresses that very clearly.

Employee in Distress

> I can't help but notice that you haven't been yourself lately. I'm not trying to pry—just to let you know I care. If I can be of any help, please don't hesitate to contact me.

Condolences

> I don't know what to say, except that my heart feels for you. Although I didn't know Nancy well, I've always heard of her devotion to you and the family and of all the wonderful work she did for charity. She will certainly be missed.

> Your friends at the office are all thinking of you and want to be of help if there is anything we can do.

> Those we love never truly leave us, for they live forever in our hearts. May the love you and [deceased] shared be of comfort to you and your family.

Loss of a Job

I just heard the news. I know this is a terrible blow to you at the moment, but try to focus on all the experience you've amassed and how you will be able to plug your talents into a company where you'll be fully appreciated.

Please let me know if there is anything I can do to help. Review your résumé? Run you through a mock interview? Be an ear? Remember, you're a winner and will land on top!

Retiree

Just think of the extra sleep you'll get in the morning. The extra rounds of golf. And the vacations you've been putting off for years. It's wonderful that you and Grace are so vital and will be able to enjoy all the activities that were so often put on hold because of your hectic schedules. Our loss is Grace's gain.

This marks a major change in your life. I, for one, welcome the extra time we'll be able to share.

Thanks for Support

To My Friends at Unitron,

When one is ill, there is plenty of time for reflecting on one's blessings. Having you as my co-worker and friend is certainly one of my blessings. I can't tell you how your good wishes and visits brightened those long, dreary days during my recovery.

I'll be back to the "old grind" within the next three weeks, wearing my three-piece suit like a smile. In the meantime, I want you all to know that your good words were a turning point in my recovery.

To love what you do and to feel that you matter—what more could anyone want!

Frank

CONGRATULATIONS

Congratulatory letters are probably the nicest to write. Take advantage of these opportunities; they are innumerable. When congratulating someone:

- be enthusiastic

- be sincere, without showing envy
- stick to the accomplishment or the occasion

Promotion

It didn't take the Maxwell Company long to recognize your talents. Eight years is an extremely short time to burn a path from Junior Salesman to Vice-President of Sales. You've worked hard, gained everyone's respect, and now you've made it to the top. Our cooperation is yours for the asking.

I know how happy you and Jack must be with the news of your promotion. It is a well-deserved step in your career. You're climbing the ladder of success so quickly, I'm getting dizzy. My best wishes for your continued success.

New Job

It's time to bid you adieu. Although I'm not happy to see you leave the organization, I know this is an important career move. The Bennett Company is lucky to have you on board. Please know that you will surely be missed by all of us here and that we are all celebrating for you.

I read in the company's newsletter about your appointment to the position of Vice President of the Penny Savings Bank. I'm sure you're excited about the challenges that await you in the new position. Lots of success and happiness in your new job.

Project Recognition or Award

The Baker project would never have been completed without your 150 percent effort during the last several months. Congratulations on the excellent work you and your team did. I know the many sacrifices you and your families made in order to bring this project to completion. Your dedication is very much appreciated.

Thanks so much for your efforts in helping us to submit the budget on time. That was quite an assignment, wasn't it? Keep up the good work.

On behalf of the entire group at Miller Life Insurance Company, I want to congratulate you on being awarded Salesman of the Year. It's very inspiring to all of your co-workers to know of your excellent performance and fine record. If you can spare the time, I'd like to take you to lunch to celebrate. I'll give you a call next week.

Civic Affairs

I read with much pleasure this morning of the honors paid to you as a result of all your efforts for the Urban Renewal program of our city. May I congratulate you. As we read the doom and gloom on a daily basis, it gives one a feeling of great confidence to know that people like you are being recognized for their attributes.

When the time comes for Marlborough (that's where I live) to renew itself, we'd be lucky to have someone with your unique talents come forward.

Dear Joe,

I've been one of your admirers for so long, and I'm extremely interested in the work you've done in AIDS research. Therefore, I'm so pleased to learn that you're joining our laboratory this summer. You'll be working with many outstanding people, and I'm confident that together we'll be able to make great progress in our research.

After you get set in your office, why don't we grab some lunch? In the meantime, if I can be of help in any way, just pick up the phone. My extension is 2261.

Fondly,

Mel

RECOMMENDING MEMBERSHIP TO AN ORGANIZATION OR CLUB

Strong Recommendation

Dear . . .

The purpose of this letter is to recommend Susan Warren for membership in Bergstein's Executives Club. It is my privilege to have known Susan for fifteen years and to have watched her career flourish. The attached biography details Susan's numerous accomplishments, as well as her contributions to several nonprofit institutions. Susan has made an outstanding contribution to the field of nursing and has a reputation for being a person who cares about her community and *does something about it.*

Susan is a wife and mother of two. She has managed to juggle her family and a distinguished nursing career with an expert sense of balance. I know of no one who would make a more suitable member of Bergstein's Executive Club, and I hope the membership will look kindly on this proposal.

Please feel free to contact me if I can add anything to facilitate Susan's membership.

Cordially,

Robin Samuel

Lukewarm Recommendation

Dear . . .

In response to your request, I am addressing this letter to the Membership Committee of Bergstein's Executives Club on behalf of my colleague, Susan Warren, who is very anxious to join. I have known Susan professionally for fifteen years and have enclosed a copy of her biography for your review.

If any members of your committee would like to discuss Ms. Warren's qualifications and her suitability for membership, please contact me.

Sincerely,

Robin Samuel

THANKING A VOLUNTEER FOR A
MAJOR PROJECT

Dear Elijahu,

Our awards banquet would never have taken place if you and your staff hadn't pitched in so eagerly. I will never be able to thank you enough for booking the room and the caterer, and for mailing out the invitations.

My staff and I thoroughly enjoyed working with you. Because of everyone's good nature and sense of humor, we got through one crisis after another. You really were a lifesaver.

I owe your staff a lunch and will call next week to set one up.

Cordially,

Leah Zimmerman

CONGRATULATING AN EMPLOYEE
FOR YEARS OF SERVICE

Dear Masha,

This is certainly a proud day for you, and it is for me and the company also. You have worked twenty-five years for Spencer's, and during all those years you have offered your talents and hard work. People with your enthusiasm and dedication are what has made Spencer's the success it is today.

Congratulations! I am proud to have you on our team. Here's wishing you another happy and healthy twenty-five years with us.

Sincerely,

Catherine Sherwood

APOLOGY

From the Desk of Sandra Morgan

Dillon,

This letter is very difficult for me to write because I realize that I have offended you.

My remark this morning was quite condescending, and I wish to offer my sincerest apology. You have my personal assurance that an incident such as this will never again occur.

I have always valued our business relationship, and I truly hope that we can put this unpleasantness behind us.

Sandra

COMMENDATIONS

AMERICAN GRAPHICS

300 Brentwood Avenue, High Point, NC 27263
(919) 887-3456   (800) 221-4667

June 10, 19—

Dear Leanna,

Thank you for being a member of our Total Quality Management Process Action Team. Each of the teams at American Graphics—Communications, Equipment, and Training—achieved remarkable results, and I would like to recognize you personally for your efforts and enthusiasm.

It is quality people like you who make American Graphics a quality company.

Sincerely,

Joseph Coughlin
President

Cushing Transportation Center
100 Milton Street
White Plains, NY 10406
(914) 345-1238

Date: September 20, 19—
To: Bruce Tessier, Vice President
From: Cheryl Cushing, President
Re: Your memo dated September 16

In response to your memo dated September 16, I recently engaged the services of Lois Lorenz and Karl Ford to produce a public relations video depicting the projects in which my company has been involved. Lois and Karl were able to take charge immediately and approached the assignment with enthusiasm and thorough professionalism.

Lois was tasked with meeting with my managers and their teams to gather information and identify visuals for the script/storyboard. She captured the essence of our missions and projects and presented them with a flair that appealed to a broad-based audience. Karl applied his talents to weaving 35 mm slides, computer-generated visuals, moving footage, and special effects into an upbeat and fluid presentation.

After viewing the video, one member of my group commented: "It's refreshing to take a moment to sit back and realize all we've accomplished and the wide range of activities in which we're involved. This video has reinforced my pride in being a member of this team."

The 20-minute video was so well received that it prompted two of my managers to have Lois and Karl produce videos for their groups. Yes, I highly recommend Lois and Karl. They are very professional in their services and produce a quality product.

Cheryl Cushing

Sheryl Lindsell Roberts

February 18, 19—

Mayor Michael P. Hogan
Marlborough City Hall
140 Main Street
Marlborough, MA 01754

Dear Mayor Hogan:

My husband and I are in the process of purchasing four acres of land in
the Wayside Inn Area. This land spans the Marlborough-Sudbury line, and
we are planning to build our home in the City of Marlborough. This has
been a very difficult transaction for a number of reasons, and I've spent a
great deal of time on the telephone with various people from the
Marlborough City Hall.

I want to commend the group of people you have working there—for they
are the most courteous and helpful group of people with whom I have
ever dealt. I had the pleasure of dealing with Steve Reid, Building Inspector; Ron White, Engineer; Ron DeSantis, Building Department; Dottie,
Building Inspector's Office; the gentleman from the Board of Health; and
a few others whose names I neglected to take.

If this is any indication of what life will be like in Marlborough, I can
hardly wait.

Sincerely,

Sheryl Roberts

Sheryl Roberts

One Bengal Lane, Salem, MA 01970 • (508)745-2616

CITY OF MARLBOROUGH
Marlborough, Massachusetts 01752

February 24, 19—

Ms. Sheryl Roberts
One Bengal Lane
Salem, Massachusetts 01970

Dear Sheryl:

Thank you for your note of February 18 regarding the various staff people
here at City Hall that you have dealt with over the past few months. With a
strong commitment to service, all our departments strive to provide a
consistent level of help to those seeking our assistance. It is unfortunate
that more people who have a good experience do not take the time to let
people know that they are appreciated.

Good luck with your project. Please feel free to contact me directly if there
is anything that I might do for you. Thank you again for your kind words;
I'll be sure to pass them on to the appropriate departments.

Sincerely,

MICHAEL P. HOGAN
Mayor

CHAPTER TEN

ETCETERA

Etcetera is generally used to connote "and so forth." There are many letters that fit into the "and so forth" category because they are not lengthy enough to have chapters of their own. Here are the *etcetera* letters discussed in this chapter.

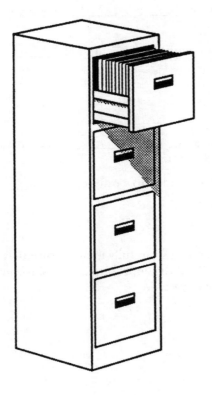

- Transmittals
- Secretary Responding to Correspondence
- Soliciting Funds
- Sexual Harassment Policy Statement
- Invitation or Meeting Announcement
- Denying an Agency an Account
- Squelching a Rumor
- Handling a Disagreement with a Co-worker
- Renewing a Membership
- Submitting a Magazine Article
- Banking
- Insurance
- Real Estate
- Law

TRANSMITTALS

Transmittal letters should accompany all reports, forms, legal documents, checks, policies, manuscripts, surveys, etc. A transmittal letter should be brief and should identify each document that is included.

Dear . . .

Enclosed is an original and copy of your 19— Federal and State income tax returns, the details of which appear below. On each of the two originals, please sign your name and date in every place you see a check mark. Then place the originals in the enclosed, pre-addressed envelopes.

Federal Income Tax Return

☑ Attach a check in the amount of $_____, made payable to the Internal Revenue Service.

☑ Due to an overpayment, you are entitled to a refund of $_____.

☑ No tax is due on your return.

State Income Tax Return

☑ Attach a check in the amount of $_____, made payable to the [State] Department of Revenue.

☑ Due to an overpayment, you are entitled to a refund of $_____.

☑ No tax is due on your return.

Please check these income tax returns carefully to make sure they are accurate and that you sign in all the appropriate places. If you have any questions, please give me a call.

Yours truly,

SKYSCRAPER CONSTRUCTION

200 Elaine Street, Wausau, WI 54401
(715) 845-3200

June 8, 19—

Ms. Christine Nicolucci
12 Joseph Lane
Wausau, WI 54401

Dear Ms. Nicolucci:

Enclosed is the list of references you requested. Feel free to contact any of these companies to inquire about our ethics, standards, and workmanship.

If we can be of any further assistance, please let us know.

Sincerely,

Anthony Michael

Enclosure

SECRETARY RESPONDING
TO CORRESPONDENCE

When an executive is gone from the office for a prolonged period of time, it is important not to let mail pile up. A secretary should acknowledge mail in a timely manner. Unless the executive knows the correspondent personally, the secretary should not divulge personal reasons (illness, vacation, etc.) for the absence. These are examples of interim responses:

> This will acknowledge receipt of your letter dated [date]. Mr. Smith will be away from the office for the remainder of the week. Your letter will be brought to his immediate attention as soon as he returns. I hope this won't cause you any inconvenience.

> I know that Mr. Smith will enjoy hearing from you. He will be away from the office until [date] and will be in touch when he returns.

SOLICITING FUNDS

Requesting a Donation

Dear Friend:

Things are rapidly changing in the health care profession, except for the funds that are so badly needed to meet the demands of tomorrow. Today's health care institutions are facing unprecedented challenges. These challenges involve ideas and programs that will offer new advances in health care.

As you know, the Get-Well Hospital has always tried to offer the community the latest in quality health care. We are completely autonomous and nonprofit and can't do it without your help. We have reached 75% of our goal for the new Heart Wing, but additional funds are badly needed. Won't you please help us reach our goal of [$____]? You will be part of a team dedicated to the development of the finest health care facility in the community.

Please put a check for whatever you can afford in the envelope that is enclosed. What could be more worthwhile?

Gratefully,

Thanking for a Donation

Dear Mr. James:

Your generous gift to the fund for the Architecture Building at Georgia Tech is very much appreciated. The Building is nearly completed, offering a wonderful addition to our campus. We have reached 90% of our goal, and contributions are still rolling in. Please visit the new Architecture Building and see how your contribution has been spent.

Thank you for your generosity, making the long-term goal of the new Architecture Building a reality!

Cordially,

ILYSSA SCHWARTZ LEUKEMIA FOUNDATION

"The capacity to care is the thing which gives life its deepest meaning"

FRONT

Ilyssa Schwartz Leukemia Foundation
P.O. Box 508 · Montville, NJ 07045

Your thoughtful remembrance will be acknowledged . . . A beautiful, specially designed card will be sent to the person or family you designate. The amount of the gift will not be disclosed.

Enclosed is my gift of ❑ $10 ❑ $15 ❑ $25 ❑ $50 ❑ $100 ❑ $500 ❑ Other_____
❑ First Time Contributor   ❑ Previous Contributor

Name of Contributor_____

Street_____

City _____ State _____ Zip _____ Phone __(   )_____

Name of Person Honored_____

❑ Memorial   ❑ Anniversary   ❑ Bar/Bat Mitzvah   ❑ Thank You
❑ Confirmation   ❑ Wedding   ❑ To Honor Parents/Other ❑ Other Occasion_____
❑ Get Well   ❑ Birthday   ❑ Holiday   ❑ Send more envelopes #___

I would like to become a member of the Ilyssa Schwartz Leukemia Foundation ❑

Please send acknowledgement to:_____

Street_____

City_____ State_____ Zip_____

Make checks payable to Ilyssa Schwartz Leukemia Foundation. 201-227-0733. All contributions are tax deductible

BACK

Dear Friend:

Ilyssa Schwartz, pre-law student at American University, was diagnosed with Acute Myelogenous Leukemia on June 1, 1991. Immediately hospitalized, Ilyssa began the first of six intensive chemotherapy protocols. For the next 265 days Ilyssa and her family, who never left her side, called Mount Sinai Medical Center home. Eight months later, this feisty young woman, who enjoyed life to the fullest, succumbed to her illness on her 23rd birthday.

Kind people everywhere, knowing of her plight and her ever mounting hospital and medical bills, came to the aid of her family with support. This support was both emotional as well as financial.

The plight of a very young child stricken with a fatal disease never fails to tug deeply at our emotions. However, if the sick person is a young adult we react differently to his or her plight. Remember: EACH OF US IS SOMEONE'S CHILD WITH THE NEED FOR LOVE AND EMOTIONAL SUPPORT. There are times when the family also needs other support, namely financial.

To honor the memory of Ilyssa, the ILYSSA SCHWARTZ LEUKEMIA FOUNDATION* has been established by both her family and friends. Joe Pesci, who knew Ilyssa, has so graciously consented to be our Honorary Chairman. Our goal is to help young adults and their families, while respecting both their dignity and privacy. All members of this foundation are volunteers - no one is salaried. Every dollar raised will be used directly for patient needs.

We have channeled our efforts to work in conjunction with Cancer Care, Inc., North Jersey Blood Center and the Saint Barnabas Medical Center. Careful research is done before any distributions are made. Your contribution will be allocated to our specially established programs.

In keeping with our motto shown above, we come to you since you are one who cares. We are asking you for a contribution to the ILYSSA SCHWARTZ LEUKEMIA FOUNDATION* which will enable us to continue our worthwhile endeavors.

WHERE DOES A FAMILY IN CRISIS GO FOR SUPPORT?   *CancerCare,Inc.·*

 We provide supplementary financial support for Cancer Care, Inc. to help leukemia patients between the ages of 18 and 40 and their families meet certain home care costs: pain medication as well as travel expenses for medical treatment. These are needs not normally covered under medical insurance.

HOW CAN WE GET MORE VOLUNTEERS TO BE TESTED FOR THE NATIONAL MARROW DONOR PROGRAM?

 We provide funding for the National Marrow Donor Program through the North Jersey Blood Center. This helps patients defray the high cost of the blood test for tissue typing which is the first step in finding a suitable donor for a "miracle match" bone marrow transplant.

WHEN A PATIENT'S HAIR FALLS OUT AS A RESULT OF RADIATION OR CHEMOTHERAPY, WHERE DO THEY GO FOR SUPPORT? SAINT BARNABAS MEDICAL CENTER

 We provide funds for the purchase of wigs at Saint Barnabas Medical Center's Clinical Cosmetology Center. This support helps those patients, whose appearance may have suffered from treatment, improve their self-image and restore their dignity.

P.O. BOX 508 · MONTVILLE · NEW JERSEY 07045 · PHONE 201-227-0733
HONORARY CHAIRMAN JOE PESCI

*Publicly supported tax qualified foundation, Sec. 501(a) (1) & Sec. 170(b) (1) (A) (V1) A11 contributions made to this foundation are tax deductible

INSIDE

May 21, 19—

Ms. Sheryl L. Roberts
1 Bengal Lane
Salem, MA 01970-6806

Dear Sheryl,

*AIDS Action
Committee of
Massachusetts, Inc.*

Going to friends' funerals is sad enough. But it's really
heartbreaking when a family member says, "If I'd only known,
I would have helped."

That's why I've worked so hard since my HIV diagnosis in 1985, encouraging my family, friends, and neighbors to understand this terrible
illness and band together to support me and each other.

None of them knows what it's like to wake up every morning feeling
like you have the flu, dreading the medicines that make you feel even
worse, not knowing whether you can make plans for next week.

But all of them are there for me on those days when I need help
managing life with AIDS. And they are there for each other as they
wrestle with the grief that someone they love will die too young.

AIDS Action is on my team, too. Volunteers like my Buddy, who sees me
through ups and downs . . . the lawyer who drafted my will . . . a
dog-walker I count on for those difficult days—they're all stars.

I'm lucky. Too many other people living with HIV are struggling all
alone. *For them, often the only place to turn is AIDS Action.*

But AIDS Action depends on the generosity of friends. I'm proud that
"Team Lodie" is raising pledges and walking next Sunday in the AIDS
pledge walk to show *how much we care about all people living with HIV.* I
just hope I'll feel well enough to be there.

I hope you, too, will join in and show again how much you care—*by
sending your most generous gift directly to AIDS Action, today.*

With friends like you on the AIDS Action team, no one needs t
be alone with HIV. Thank you from all of us.

*131 Clarendon Street
Boston, MA 02116*

617.437.6200
Fax *617.437.6445*

AIDS Action Hotline
617.536.7733
MA: *1.800.235.2331*

Sincerely,

Jay Lodie

Jay Lodie

Letter courtesy of Nancy Greenhouse, *Greenhouse Direct.*

July 7, 19—

Ms Sheryl L. Roberts
1 Bengal Lane
Salem, MA 01970

*AIDS Action
Committee of
Massachusetts. Inc.*

Dear Ms. Roberts,

Thank you for your gift of $50 to the AIDS Action Committee.

On behalf of the AIDS Action family—clients, volunteers and staff—I want to thank you for your contribution to our work. Without your generous support, we wouldn't be able to provide the services we do for people living with HIV and those who love and care for them.

Your gift helps us combat AIDS through client services, targeted education and outreach programs, AIDS Action's hotlines, and Speakers Bureau. With your help, our public policy team continues to fight for compassionate laws that protect people with AIDS and for adequate resources to address the epidemic.

Although the fight is far from over, we are making progress. We appreciate your gift.

Sincerely yours,

Larry

Larry Kessler
Executive Director

Letter courtesy of Nancy Greenhouse, *Greenhouse Direct*.

*131 Clarendon Street
Boston. MA 02116*

617.437.6200
Fax 617.437.6445

AIDS Action Hotline
617.536.7733
MA: 1.800.235.2331

FRIENDSHIP FUND
P.O. Box 3450
Benton Harbor, MI 49023-3450

May 1, 19—

Dear Friend,

The Friendship Fund is starting its annual drive on June 1. We hope you will once again make a contribution to this worthwhile cause.

In the past, your company has been one of the leaders in this drive, with its employees contributing 2% of their incomes. Naturally, we realize that your employees' dollars aren't stretching as far as they used to; ours aren't either. Please let us count on your generosity again this year; it will make the difference to so many who are in need. This year we are asking that each company open its heart and match the contribution of its employees.

Your tax-deductible check can be made payable to the Friendship Fund. Just place your check in the self-addressed envelope that is enclosed and know that you are helping members of the community who so desperately need the care we help to provide. Thank you so much for your continued support.

Gratefully yours,

Dolores Ramsey

SEXUAL HARASSMENT
POLICY STATEMENT

It is illegal to harass anyone or make anyone feel uncomfortable in the workplace. Therefore, companies across the nation are issuing policy statements that are being distributed to employees and/or placed on bulletin boards. A policy statement of this nature should contain:

- a definition of sexual harassment

- the fact that sexual harassment is illegal

- procedures to be followed if one has been victimized

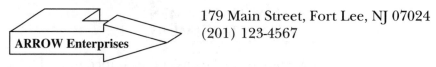

179 Main Street, Fort Lee, NJ 07024
(201) 123-4567

Date: Februry 3, 19—
To: All Employees
From: Human Resources
Re: Arrow's Sexual Harassment Policy

Arrow Enterprises has provided workplace guidelines for preventing and addressing sexual harassment. It has come to our attention recently that these guidelines need additional clarification.

What Is Sexual Harassment?
Sexual harassment at work occurs whenever unwelcome conduct—on the basis of gender—affects an employee's job. There two types:

1. When anyone in authority threatens the employee with termination, demotion, intimidation, etc., for refusing sexual advances.

2. When anyone creates an abusive or hostile work environment or interferes with the employee's job performance through words or action because of the victim's gender.

Sexual harassment is illegal and will not be tolerated at Arrow. Further, any employee who is found to have committed sexual harassment will be subject to severe disciplinary action, which could include termination.

What Is a Hostile Work Environment?
A hostile work environment is created by unwelcome conduct, such as:

- discussing sexual activities

- unnecessary touching

- commenting on physical attributes

- telling off-color jokes

- displaying sexually aggressive pictures, calendars, or photos

- using demeaning or inappropriate terms and nicknames

- using suggestive gestures

- ostracizing employees because of gender

- using crude or offensive language

Complaint Procedures and Responsibilities

Supervisors are responsible for assisting in preventing sexual harassment by maintaining a productive work environment. Should a report of harassment occur in their work areas, supervisors are responsible for assisting in the investigation and resolution of the complaint.

An employee who feels victimized by an act of harassment should immediately report the incident to his/her immediate supervisor. If the immediate supervisor is the source of the harassment, discuss the incident(s) with the supervisor's manager or with someone in the Human Resources Department. All complaints will be treated with respect and confidentiality. Further, no employee will be subject to any form of retaliation or discipline for pursuing a sexual harassment complaint.

INVITATION OR MEETING ANNOUNCEMENT

Whether you are planning a business meeting, a management seminar, or a get-together, it is important to determine whether the occasion can be categorized as formal or informal so you will know what kind of invitation to send out. Formal gatherings can warrant engraved invitations, while in-house meeting announcements warrant simple memos.

When people's attendance is requested, they should be given adequate notice—a week or ten days. If you do not give adequate notification, recipients may have full calendars. If you give notification too far in advance, they may forget. For large gatherings, or those where people must make special arrangements, more time is required. An invitation or meeting announcement should contain:

- exact time, date, and place

- why the meeting is taking place

- duration of the meeting

- an agenda

- directions, if applicable

> The next regular meeting of the Fanuel Lake Association will be held in the Community Meeting Room at 8 PM sharp on Tuesday, March 16.
>
> Mayor John Smith will be speaking on new laws that will affect condominium owners. The presentation should last about one hour and will be followed by a question and answer period. Please plan to attend.

> We heard your interesting talk at the Simmons dinner meeting last month and regretted that many of our sales staff weren't there to absorb your piquant point of view.
>
> We'd very much like you to address our sales staff at the next sales meeting which will be held at our headquarters at one o'clock on Thursday, September 12, 19—. If it is possible for you to be with us, please let us know within the next two weeks so we can make all the arrangements.

SULLIVAN & KARP, INC., has just moved its offices
to 600 Main Street, Centertown, SC 29212.
Our new phone number is (803) 345-6000.

Please circle June 5 on your calendar and plan to stop by
for our office-warming celebration. We'll be serving
cocktails from six until nine in the evening.

It is our way of saying "thank you" to all our clients for our
many years of success in the community.

DENYING AN AGENCY AN ACCOUNT

Agencies go through harrowing experiences when they submit proposals. There are endless rounds of telephone calls, meetings, and presentation materials—to say nothing of the tremendous stress waiting to find out whether they are *winners* or *also-rans*. Corporate America is tough when it comes to getting their proposals submitted on time, but they are not always timely or considerate with their responses.

When an agency has worked hard to put together a proposal, it deserves a telephone call followed with a letter the day the decision is made. When denying an agency an account, be honest with your reason and timely with your reply. At all costs, the recipient must be able to save face.

 **BENGAL ASSOCIATES**
300 California Street, Suite 2
Berkeley, CA 94703
(415) 123-4567

January 5, 19—

Ms. Valerie Nashua
Nashua & Associates
One Darth Parkway
Ludlow, CO 80304

Dear Ms. Nashua:

As I mentioned to you on the phone yesterday, the Vice President has selected [agency] to handle the account. This was a very difficult decision to make because you are all such highly qualified candidates. The decision finally came down to the fact that [agency] has had a lot more experience in the telecommunications marketplace.

We all know what an outstanding job you would have done and appreciate all the time and creativity that went into your presentation. This is not the last time we will be approaching you for a project, and perhaps the next time things will work out more favorably for you.

Please thank your entire team and commend them on a job well done. I offer my personal wishes for your continued success.

Sincerely,

Richard McCusker
Director of Public Relations

SQUELCHING A RUMOR

MEMORANDUM

Date: November 1, 19—
To: All Staff Members
From: Jon Allen, President
Re: Company Merger

If rumors are the "information virus," here's the anti-dote. I'd like to set the record straight. Perhaps you have heard rumors of all sorts to the effect that the company is going out of business, is being sold, or is merging. Well, I am pleased to tell you that the last is true. We are merging.

Effective January 1, we will become a wholly owned subsidiary of ACME, Inc., of Dallas, Texas. Principals at ACME have asked me to let you know of their sincere intentions to continue operating this division on a autonomous basis and to **retain all the employees** who are currently on the payroll.

There are many benefits to be gained by the merger, and I would like to inform you of them personally. There will be a company-wide meeting in the auditorium on Monday, November 8, 19—, at noon. The meeting will be over lunch (provided by ACME), and members of the ACME team will be on hand to personally answer any questions.

I'm sure that you'll approve of the merger wholeheartedly once you understand what we all have to gain. I look forward to seeing each of you at the luncheon on November 8.

Jon

HANDLING A DISAGREEMENT
WITH A CO-WORKER

Ed,

I've always enjoyed our working relationship, as I have a lot of respect for your creative and professional ability. However, I'm having an increasingly difficult time working with you and would like to clear the air.

It appears that each time I ask you to make a change—whether it's initiated by me or the sponsor—you get very defensive and sometimes abusive. At some level, I understand your defensiveness. As a creative person myself, I take a lot of pride in my ideas and hope that everyone will be as enthusiastic about them as I. And, yes, I am often disappointed when they aren't. However, we are all professionals and must respect and consider the ideas and opinions of others.

I want to renew the working relationship we've shared in the past, but we must be able to work as a team and not let our egos get in the way of that team effort. I'm sure you'll agree.

Rob

RENEWING A MEMBERSHIP

We hope you'll renew your membership!

We miss you as a member. The enclosed renewal notice is sent with the club's gratitude for your past membership and with the hope that you'll rejoin us at this time.

We want you to know that dues will increase as of September 1, and because of your past membership we invite you to rejoin now to qualify for the current rates.

We look forward to renewing your membership and thank you for your continued interest.

Leah Todd

SUBMITTING A MAGAZINE ARTICLE

Perhaps you have a story waiting to be born or a professional idea, hint, or experience waiting to be shared. So you write an article. (It should be double spaced with 1" margins all around.) Your first byline will be a landmark accomplishment and a springboard to other opportunities. "How do I go about getting an article published?" you ask.

Query Letter

- *Become familiar with the magazine marketplace.* Obtain a copy of the *Writer's Market.* It is published annually and lists a wide array of publications. Also, visit stores that sell magazines and know what types of articles your target magazines contain.

- *Send a query letter to each appropriate magazine editor.* It should be limited to one page and should:

  —briefly explain the structure of the article

  —list your qualifications for writing the article

  —mention the number of words in the article

  —if applicable, indicate whether or not photographs are available

- *Send with each query letter a means by which the editor can respond.*

  You can do this in one of two ways: Send (1) the article and an SASE (self-addressed, stamped envelope) with adequate return postage, or (2) a postal card on which the editor can indicate his/her interest in seeing the article.

[ ]   Yes, I would like to see a copy of your article entitled ". . . ."

[ ]   No thank you, your article doesn't meet our current needs.

Name of Magazine

Back of Postal Card

Your name
Address
City, State ZIP

Front of Postal Card

MASHA NICOLE
14 Ivy Lane
Spring Valley, New York 10977
(914) 356-7654

June 20, 19—

Ms. Martha Rones, Editor
Life Styles Magazine
100 Mitchell Drive
New York, NY 10020

Dear Ms. Rones:

I would like to propose an article entitled "Shoulder to Shoulder" that should be of great interest to your readers. I was prompted to write this article after having visited Ellis Island recently. I thought of the 12 million immigrants processed through the Island and the wealth of hopes and dreams they brought with them. When I returned home, I was bombarded with a sharp contrast. The news that evening was dominated by race riots, gay bashing, and other acts against minorities. "Where will this end?" I wondered. And what ever happened to the words ". . . with liberty and justice for all?"

As an established author who has had many professional books and magazine articles published, I put many of my thoughts and feelings on paper. "Shoulder to Shoulder," which contains approximately 1200 words, deals with the following theme: Somehow the lens through which we look at life has become clouded. In a nation that has always drawn its greatness from diversity, why must we focus hate on those who are different? The journey to acceptance is a long and arduous struggle for many.

I hope you will be interested in reading "Shoulder to Shoulder" with a view toward publishing it in *Life Styles* magazine. Please indicate on the enclosed postal card your interest in reading this article.

Sincerely,

Masha Nicole

Enc.

Follow-up Letter

Although it can take up to several months, most editors will respond. If an editor wants to see a copy of your article, the letter in which you enclose it should be brief and to the point. Do not make another sales pitch; at this point the article must stand on its own merit. There is no need to send an SASE because the article is now being requested.

> Enclosed is my article entitled "Shoulder to Shoulder," which you requested to see. I look forward to hearing from you at your earliest convenience.

BANKING

Correcting a Bank Error

Dear . . .

Subject: Account No. 345 345 55

Enclosed is a deposit receipt for interest on the $5,000 at $2\frac{1}{4}$ % for 24 days. As we discussed during our conversation this morning, this should correct the inaccuracy in your account.

I apologize for the error and for any inconvenience it has caused. We have taken appropriate action to see that a problem such as this does not happen again.

We value you as a customer and appreciate your loyalty to [bank]. If I can be of further assistance now or in the future, please don't hesitate to call me.

Sincerely,

Opening a New Account

Dear . . .

Thank you for choosing [bank] as the new home for your checking account. We will try to provide you with the kind of service that will maintain the confidence you have shown in us.

Enclosed is a supply of temporary checks along with a temporary check register. Your supply of 1000 personalized checks should reach you within the next two weeks. I will be happy to personally service your needs on this account at any time.

Also enclosed is a brochure detailing some of [bank's] other services. If I can be of help in any way, please give me a call.

Cordially,

INSURANCE

Notice of Premium Due (Form Letter)

Date:
Policy No.
Date Due:
Amount Due:
Type of Coverage:

JUST A REMINDER!

The premium on your policy is twenty days past due. If your check is in the mail, just disregard this notice. If not, please drop it in the mail today to avoid a lapse in your coverage.

If I can be of help with this policy or with any other type of insurance coverage, please call me.

Sincerely,

Notice of Policy Discontinuation (Form Letter)

Date:
Policy No.
Expiration Date:

Dear Policyholder:

In the interest of all our policyholders, we sometimes find it necessary to discontinue individual policies. It is always with deep regret that we do this.

In accordance with the provisions of the policy contract, we will not be able to renew the above policy as of 12:01 AM, standard time, on the expiration date shown above. This is necessary for the following reasons:

-
-

If you are unable to obtain Fire and Extended Coverage Insurance on your property from another company, you may be eligible for this insurance through the Property Insurance Placement Facility in your state. For further information, please contact your insurance agent or broker.

It was a pleasure dealing with you over the last several years, and again we regret having to take this course of action.

Sincerely,

REAL ESTATE

Extending a Listing

Dear . . .

Re: Renewal of Real Estate Listing

Despite a sluggish market, the activity on your home has been increasing. I am confident that we will be successful in a sale in the near future.

We have made our best efforts on your behalf because we realize how important this sale is to you. During the next few months we will continue to place advertisements in prominent real estate publications, hold open houses, and provide updated information to the Multiple Listing System.

As you know, your listing will expire next month. I've enclosed a renewal form extending your listing for an additional six months. Please sign the form and return it to me in the enclosed envelope, so that we can continue our best efforts without interruption.

Cordially,

David

David Dworkin

Thank you for the confidence you have shown in me.

Client Referral

Dear . . .

Thank you so much for referring [name] to me. As referrals are an important part of my business, I always appreciate the confidence shown in me.

You can be assured that [name] will receive my utmost attention to the sale of their beautiful home.

Cordially,

David

David Dworkin

LAW

Notification of Settlement (Form Letter)

Dear

Re: Settlement
      address
      From . . . To

We are pleased to advise you that settlement on the above-captioned property has been scheduled as follows:

Date:
Time:
Place:

It will be necessary for both of you to be present promptly at the scheduled time and place to sign the necessary papers.

If either of you has been previously married, please bring a copy of your divorce decree and settlement.

Moneys due over the amount of $1,000 should be taken to settlement in cash or certified check. Smaller sums can be paid by personal check. Please see the attached schedule, which details all the moneys for which you will be responsible.

It will be necessary for you to have a Homeowners Fire Insurance Policy at the time of final settlement. Also, please make arrangements with your utility companies to switch the gas, electric, and water.

If you have any questions, please don't hesitate to call me.

                              Very truly yours,

Enclosure

SUE ANN COURT
Attorney at Law
5 North Madison Avenue
Spring Valley, NY 10977
(914) 356-6780

May 12, 19—

Mr. and Mrs. Anthony Cosenza
23 Joel Place
Monsey, NY 10952

Dear Tony and Raye:

Re: Cosenza v. Sheridan

Joseph N. Wheeler, attorney for the defendant in the above-captioned matter, has requested that your deposition be taken at my office on June 2, 19— at 10 AM.

Let me point out that a deposition is an informal proceeding. Mr. Wheeler will ask you questions pertaining to several issues surrounding this case. His questions and your answers will be taken down by a court reporter and transcribed in booklet form. All statements will be taken under oath and may be used if we go to trial.

Please call me for an appointment before the date of the deposition so that we can review all the issues regarding this case.

Sincerely,

Sue Ann Court

PART·III

REFERENCE SECTION

CHAPTER ELEVEN

PROOFREADING

Due ewe sea any mistakes hear?

Quality control is a term that has been much bandied about lately. It has been used in the automobile industry, the high-tech industry, and in most industries where products are manufactured for consumer use.

As a letter writer, you control the quality of your letter. Proofreading is not an innate talent; it is a skill—a skill that can be learned and developed.

WHAT TO LOOK FOR

- Scan the overall letter to be certain the formatting and styling are correct. (Example: If you used the modified block style, are the date, complimentary closing, and signature line indented?)

- Double check the spelling of all names, initials, and any numbers or statistical information.

- Pay attention to small words (as, in, an, it, if) because they are often overlooked.

- Be aware of homonyms (*their* and *there, its* and *it's*).

- Check the continuity of all numbering schemes.

- Be aware of transpositions, word repetition, hyphenations, and spacing.

Hint: Spelling can be double checked by reading from right to left or from bottom to top.

LETTING YOUR COMPUTER DO THE WORK?

If you use computer software that comes with a spell checker and grammar checker, your job will certainly be simplified. But I must caution you about becoming too dependent on your computer because there is nothing that can replace human intervention. In the sentence "Due ewe sea any mistakes hear?" the spell checker and grammar checker would not find any mistakes.

Also, one small word, incorrectly typed, can completely alter the meaning of a sentence. Note the difference in the sentences below, neither of which would be detected as having an error.

I will *not* be able to go to the meeting.

I will *now* be able to go to the meeting.

CHAPTER TWELVE

PUNCTUATION

Execution; impossible to be sent to Siberia.

Execution impossible; to be sent to Siberia.

If you will note the difference in meaning between the two sentences above, you will realize the vital role punctuation plays in communicating clear and accurate messages. The following guidelines will clarify many of the punctuation problems with which you may be having difficulty.

COMMAS

The comma (,) is the most misused mark of punctuation. Its main purpose is to help the reader properly interpret the meaning of a sentence.

Addresses and Dates

Use commas between items in an address or date.

> We are moving our headquarters to 24 Besen Parkway, New York, New York, next month. (If the ZIP code were used in this example, a comma would not be placed after the state but would follow the ZIP.)

> On Sunday, August 15, 19—, Marc will be seventeen.

When using the month and year only, either surround the year with commas or omit them completely.

> In August, 19—, Marc will be seventeen.
> In August 19— Marc will be seventeen.

Appositives

Use commas to set off expressions that explain the preceding word, name, or phrase.

> Lafayette Avenue, our town's main street, is closed for repair.
>
> Mr. Weston, our representative, is waiting to see you.
>
> Mr. Weston, of Harkness Brothers, is waiting to see you.
>
> My only sister, Susan, has been accepted at West Point.

Conjunctions

Use a comma before a conjunction (*and, but, for, or, nor, yet*) provided the conjunction joins two independent clauses that could otherwise be complete sentences.

> George will not be here at ten but will arrive at eleven. (independent and dependent)
>
> George will not be here at ten, but he will arrive at eleven. (independent and independent)

Direct Address

Use commas to set off words that directly address the person to whom you are speaking either by name, title, or relationship.

> Mr. Green, please send me a copy of that letter.
>
> Please send me a copy of that letter, Mr. Green.
>
> Let me tell you, fellow members, what the committee has done.

Introductory Clauses

Use a comma after an introductory clause. Note that an introductory clause will always be followed by what could be a complete sentence. (Some key words are *if, since, because, when, while, as, unless, provided, after,* and *before.*)

> When we finish the chapter, we will have a test.
>
> Because you came late, you will have to stay late.
>
> Unless you call, I will assume you are coming.
>
> If I hear from him, I will notify you.

Use a comma to set off an independent introductory expression that serves as an interjection.

No, I do not think he is correct.

In fact, I do not think anyone knows the answer.

You know, he may have been too shy to ask.

Nonrestrictive and Restrictive Elements

Use commas to set off expressions that if omitted would not change or destroy the meaning of the sentence.

The woman who just entered is my sister. (Restrictive. *Who just entered* identifies which woman.)

My sister, who is wearing a red coat, is an accountant. (Nonrestrictive. *Who is wearing a red coat* describes but does not change the meaning of the subject *sister.*)

This magazine, *Newsweek,* is very informative. (Nonrestrictive. *Newsweek* describes the subject, *magazine,* by giving its name but does not change the meaning of the sentence.)

The magazine *Newsweek* is very informative. (Restrictive. Here the name of the magazine is vital to the meaning of the sentence. The speaker or writer limits, or *restricts,* the quality of being *very informative* to this one magazine in a sentence that indicates a consideration of many or all magazines.)

Parenthetical Expressions

Use commas to set off a word, phrase, or clause that interrupts the natural flow of the sentence.

accordingly	in brief
as a consequence	in fact
as a result	it has been said
as a rule	it seems
as well as	I understand
as you know	moreover
by the way	nevertheless
for example	of course
however	on the contrary
I believe	on the other hand
if any	therefore
if necessary	to be sure
in addition	together with

We have, I believe, two days left.

Mr. Smith, however, will be leaving early.

We will, nevertheless, proceed as scheduled.

If any of the expressions above are used in a manner that will not interrupt the natural flow of the sentence, do not use commas.

However experienced he may be, he will not qualify for the position. (*However* is part of the introductory phrase.)

Quotations

Use commas to identify a person who is being directly quoted.

"I will not arrive until much later," he said.

He said, "I will not arrive until much later."

The comma and period at the end of quoted material always go *inside* the quotation mark.

Series

Use commas to separate a series of three or more items unless a conjunction is placed between each.

He enjoys reading and swimming. (two items)

He enjoys reading, swimming, and bowling. (three items)

He enjoys reading and swimming and bowling. (conjunctions)

In a sentence like the second example above, a comma should be placed before the final conjunction to avoid misreading. Do not use a comma before the final *and* or ampersand symbol (&) within the name of a company.

He is a member of Gold, Smith & Weston.

Titles, Degrees, and Abbreviations

Use commas to set off abbreviations, titles, and degrees that follow a name. Commas are usually placed before *Inc.* and *Ltd.*

Thomas James, Jr., is our newly elected chairman.

Max Lorenz, C.P.A., will be our guest speaker.

ABC Realty Co., Inc., is moving to the South.

Walter McNicholas, Esq., is a promising attorney.

If you use *Esq.* after the name of an attorney or *M.D.* after the name of a doctor, drop the prefixes *Mr., Dr.,* etc.

Roman numerals following a person's name are not set off with commas.

Thomas James II is our newly elected chairman.

Verbals

Use a comma following an introductory verbal phrase (a phrase beginning with an infinitive or with a verb ending *ed* or *ing*) when it is used to modify the remainder of the sentence.

To prove his point, he checked the reference book.

Provoked, he slammed the door behind him.

Lacking confidence, the boy did not enter the contest.

Miscellaneous

1. Use commas to set off adjectives that follow the noun they are modifying.

   The cashier, frustrated and exhausted, located the error.

2. Use commas to set off contrasting expressions such as *not, never, seldom.*

   I saw him in March, not April.

   He always teaches sociology, never psychology.

3. Use a comma to divide a sentence that starts as a statement and ends as a question.

   You will call him, won't you? (This type of sentence will always end with a question mark.)

4. Use commas to separate items in reference works.

   You will find that information in Volume III, Chapter 2, page 12, line 2.

5. Use commas to separate words that are repeated for emphasis.

   He told me that story many, many times.

6. Use commas to clarify numerals that have four or more digits.

   $1,000   4,356 votes   12,000 words

Exceptions include telephone numbers, years, serial numbers, ZIP codes, invoice numbers, policy numbers, and the like.

    352-8198   Policy No. 110285641   10952 (ZIP)

7. Use commas in sentences that would be confusing if they were omitted.

> Only one week before, I had lunch with him. (Without the comma, you would have a sentence fragment.)

8. Use commas to indicate that readily understood words have been omitted.

> Theodore will be given $500; Susan, $300; and Bob, $200. (After *Susan* and after *Bob*, the words *will be given* have been omitted.)

9. Use a comma after the complimentary closing of a letter, except when you are using open punctuation. (Note that only the first word of the complimentary closing is capitalized.)

> Sincerely yours,   Respectfully yours,
>
> Very truly yours,   Cordially yours,

10. Use a comma to separate two sets of figures that are not related.

> Since 1958, 500 machines have been sold.

11. Use a comma after inverted names such as on a list or in a file.

> Coleman, Russell (*Russell* is the first name.)

12. Use a comma to separate a phrase from the rest of the sentence when the phrase is inverted or taken out of its natural order.

> For me, it will mean more work and less pay.

13. Use a comma to separate two adjectives in a series, provided the word *and* could be used between the two.

> She is an intelligent, thoughtful person. (The word *and* could be placed between: *intelligent and thoughtful.*)

> These three old manual typewriters are in need of repair. (The word *and* could not logically be placed between *three old manual.*)

SEMICOLONS

The semicolon (;) has often been referred to as a weak period or a strong comma. It is a useful mark of punctuation, but it should be used sparingly.

1. Use a semicolon to separate independent clauses in a compound sentence when no conjunction is used to join the clauses.

> You need not send any money now; we will bill you later. (Two independent clauses: *You need not send any money now. We will bill you later.*)

> You need not send any money, for we will bill you later. (When a conjunction is used, a comma will separate the clauses.)

2. Use a semicolon to separate independent clauses joined by a conjunction (such as *and, but, or, nor*) if two or more commas are used in either clause and if the semicolon will prevent misreading.

> I thought I had met everyone in your family; but James, the youngest, told me that you have a sister who lives in Canada.

> I like red, blue, and green; but she likes brown, black, and rust.

3. Use a semicolon between coordinate clauses of a compound sentence when they are joined by transitional (parenthetical) words and phrases. (Check the list of parenthetical expressions given in the "Commas" section of this chapter.)

> The jury has been deliberating for two days; however, they have not reached a decision.

> President Smith has approved a new tax cut; therefore, we should start to see more money in our paychecks.

4. Use a semicolon to separate items in a series when the items themselves contain commas.

> He was available on Monday, January 5; Tuesday, January 6; and Wednesday, January 7.

> I will be giving special awards to Alma Kuhn, secretary; Warren Bergstein, accountant; and Fran Haber, teacher.

5. Use a semicolon before expressions such as *for example, that is, for instance, that is to say,* or *namely*.

The paint is available in three colors; namely, red, blue, and beige.

Many of our policies will change this year; for example, our salespeople will be paid on a commission basis.

COLONS

The colon (:) indicates the strongest possible break in a sentence and often draws the reader's attention to that which follows.

1. Use a colon after a formal introduction that includes (or implies) the phrase *the following.*

   You should know how to use the following office machines: a computer, a fax, and a photostat.

   We expect to open branch offices in each of these states: California, Nevada, and Oregon. (*The following* is implied.)

   You should not use a colon after the main verb in a sentence.

   Her most difficult subjects are English, science, and mathematics. (*Are* is the main verb.)

2. Use a colon to introduce a long direct quotation.

   Congressman Gilroy said: "I know the importance of winning, but it is not worth your while to get yourself involved in that scheme."

3. Use a colon after a statement that introduces an explanation or an example.

   My final recommendation is this: Do not delay.

4. Use a colon after the salutation of a business letter unless you are using open punctuation.

   Gentlemen: Dear Mr. Jones:
   Dear Sir: My dear Miss Smith:

5. Use a colon to separate hours and minutes when expressed in figures. Omit the *:00* when expressing time as an even clock hour.

   4:30 p.m.   2:45 a.m.
   3 p.m.   5 p.m.

DASHES

The em-dash (—) is a very emphatic mark of punctuation used for emphasis or visual effect. Use it sparingly, because the overuse of it diminishes its effect. When typing the em-dash, do not leave a space before or after.

1. Use em-dashes to set off a parenthetical expression or an appositive that you want to emphasize.

   > Have you attended a convention in New Jersey's most famous resort—Atlantic City? (instead of comma)

   > The book—in case you are interested—is very informative.

2. Use an em-dash before a word (such as *these, any, all, each*) that sums up a preceding series.

   > Pies, cheesecakes, and tarts—these are our specialties.

   > Lynne Sullivan, Janice Teisch, and Ann Kraft—these are my friends from school.

3. Use an em-dash to indicate a summarizing thought or an afterthought added to the end of a sentence.

   > That course was a big help to me—I liked it.

   > I am sure that was not an easy decision—not even for you. (more emphasis than a comma)

4. Use an em-dash before the name of an author or work that follows adirect quotation and gives its source.

   > "Ask not what your country can do for you. Ask what you can do for your country."—John F. Kennedy

   > "English is undoubtedly the most important of the world's languages at the present time."—*Webster's New Collegiate Dictionary*

5. Use em-dashes to emphasize an independent clause that has abruptly interrupted the main thought of a sentence.

   > I was certain that our manager—he more than anyone else I know—would have recommended Jim for that promotion.

PARENTHESES

Parentheses ( ) are used in somewhat the same fashion as em-dashes, only they tend to de-emphasize the conveyed message. The degree of emphasis to be conveyed is the choice of the writer.

1. Use parentheses to set off parenthetical expressions or appositives that you want to de-emphasize.

   She returned to New York (her favorite city) for her vacation.

2. Use parentheses to set off references to charts, pages, diagrams, illustrations, chapters of books, etc.

   The section on philosophy (pages 200–260) should be very helpful to you.

3. Parentheses may be used to enclose numerals or letters that precede items in a series that are in sentence form.

   The countries to be visited are (1) England, (2) France, (3) Italy, and (4) Spain.

   For lists in columns, any of the following forms may be used:

1)	(1)	1	1.
2)	(2)	2	2.
3)	(3)	3	3.

4. Use parentheses in formal writing, such as legal documents, when the writer wants to use both the spelled out number and the written number.

   The Purchaser agrees to pay to the Seller the sum of ONE THOUSAND and 00/100 DOLLARS ($1,000.00).

5. If the item in parentheses falls inside the sentence, the sentence punctuation should be placed outside the parentheses.

   Stationery often measures 8½ by 11 inches (216 by 279 millimeters).

   When you call (hopefully today), I should have the answer.

6. If the item in parentheses is a complete sentence, the mark of punctuation will go inside the parentheses.

   Dr. Harold Siegelbaum is a gynecologist. (Dr. Louis Lefkowitz is a gynecologist and obstetrician.)

BRACKETS

1. Use brackets [ ] in quoted material to enclose anything added by someone other than the writer or speaker.

   He said, "The length of the trial [from June 15 to September 16] caused great inconvenience to the jurors."

2. Use brackets to enclose parenthetical information within a larger parenthesis.

   Your order (which included a ream of paper and a dozen pencils [markers are unavailable]) was delivered on Monday.

   Keep in mind that brackets are rarely used in business writing. They are generally found in printed material.

UNDERSCORES

1. Use an underscore (___) to set off the titles of books, magazines, newspapers, pamphlets, brochures, long poems, movies, plays, and other literary works.

   I read <u>The New York Times</u> every day.

   An alternative is to completely capitalize the title or italicize it.

   I read THE NEW YORK TIMES every day.

2. Use underscores with foreign expressions that may be unfamiliar to the reader.

   The attorney introduced <u>prima facie</u> evidence.

QUOTATION MARKS

Quotation marks (" ") are extremely important marks of punctuation and must be used properly.

1. Use quotation marks to enclose material that is directly quoted; that is, the exact words of what was originally said or written.

   "I saw your advertisement in the newspaper," he said.

   Do not put quotation marks around an indirect quotation; that is, a rewording of the original statement.

   He said that he had seen your advertisement in the newspaper.

2. Use quotation marks to enclose titles of articles, short poems, lectures or topics, paintings, short stories, or chapter names of books.

> In *Webster's Legal Secretaries Handbook* there is a very informative chapter entitled "Preparing and Typewriting Client Documents."

3. Unless otherwise punctuated, use quotation marks to set off words or phrases introduced by any of the following expressions: *the word, the term, known as, marked, termed, called, entitled.*

> The check was marked "canceled."

4. Use quotation marks around familiar words used in an unusual or unconventional manner.

> My brother thinks he is "hot stuff."

5. Use single quotation marks to set off a quotation that appears within a quotation.

> The student asked, "How do I spell the word 'accommodate'?"

6. When quoting lengthy material, place the quotation mark at the beginning of each paragraph and at the end of the final paragraph only.

> "_____
> _____.
> "_____
> _____."

Quotation Marks and Other Punctuation

1. Always place the period and comma *inside* the quotes.

> He commented, "They already left."
>
> "They already left," he commented.

2. Always place the semicolon and colon *outside* the quotes.

> He said, "I will see you about noon"; however, it is already one.

3. A question mark and exclamation point will go inside the quoted material when it applies to the quoted material *only*. It will go outside when it applies to the entire sentence.

She asked, "Did you enjoy your trip?" (The quoted material alone is the question, not the entire sentence.)

Why did you call me "impossible"? (The entire sentence is a question.)

ELLIPSES

Use an ellipsis, spoken of as three points, (. . .) to indicate what words are being omitted from the original quoted material. Space once before, between, and after each period. If indicating the omission of the end of a sentence, a complete sentence, or more, use a period followed by three points of ellipsis (. . . .).

> "Let everyone mind his own business, and endeavor to be what he was made. . . . If a man does not keep pace with his companions, perhaps it is because he hears a different drummer. Let him step to the music which he hears, however measured or far away."
>
> —Thoreau

PERIODS

The period (.) is probably the most common punctuation mark.

1. Use the period at the conclusion of a statement, a request (even when phrased politely as a question), or a command.

    I very much appreciate your consideration.
    May I hear from you at your earliest convenience. (a polite request)

2. Use the period in writing some abbreviations. (Many abbreviations are now being used without the period.)

Dr.	FBI	Mrs.	YMCA	Ph.D.	NAACP
Inc.	NATO	Co.	TVA	a.m.	CIA

    When a sentence ends with an abbreviation, one period is used which represents both the abbreviation and the end of the sentence.

    I purchased my sofa from A & D Interiors, Inc.

3. The period is used as a decimal point.

    Our profits have increased by 13.5 percent.

4. Use the period to separate dollars from cents.

    I purchased the blouse for $28.50.

QUESTION MARKS

1. Use a question mark to conclude a direct question.

    When may we expect you?

2. Use a question mark after each question in a series of short questions that relate to the same subject and verb.

    Can you join us on March 16? March 17? March 18?

3. Use a question mark when a sentence begins as a statement and ends as a question.

    You made the delivery, didn't you?

4. Use a question mark in parentheses to indicate uncertainty about a stated fact.

    You ordered ten (?) copies of the book.

5. If a question ends with an abbreviation, place the question mark after the period.

    Did you purchase that at ABC Stores, Inc.?

EXCLAMATION POINTS

The exclamation point (!) is used after a word or group of words that express strong feelings (such as anger, relief, fear, excitement, surprise).

    That is an absolutely incredible story!

    "Look out!" the man shouted.

APOSTROPHES

The apostrophe (') is used primarily to indicate an omission or to show possession.

1. Use an apostrophe to indicate that there has been an omission in a number or a word.

    '89 (1989)   didn't (did not)   I've (I have)

    In formal writing, however, it is proper to avoid contractions, when possible.

    Formal: I will call as soon as I have returned.
    Informal: I'll call as soon as I've returned.

2. Form the possessive of a singular noun by adding an apostrophe and an *s.*

the cat's meow	the baby's bottle
Sue's coat	Mr. Jones's car
your boss's desk	the lady's umbrella

3. Form the possessive of a plural noun that ends in *s* by adding an apostrophe only.

two cats' food	the babies' bottles
the girls' coats	the Joneses' car
your bosses' desks	the ladies' umbrellas

4. Form the possessive of an irregular plural noun (one that does not end in *s*) by adding an apostrophe and an *s.*

your teeth's condition	children's toys
women's hats	oxen's hoofs
salespeople's commissions	foremen's influence

5. Use the apostrophe in common expressions referring to time, distance, value, or measurement.

yesterday's news	a moment's notice
a month's vacation	three months' vacation
five miles' distance	a year's salary

6. Use the apostrophe after the period in order to make an abbreviation possessive.

The M.B.A.'s thesis
ABC Realty Co.'s contracts
the M.D.'s opinion

7. Use the apostrophe to indicate possession at the end of a compound word.

sister-in-law's car	the secretary treasurer's report
sisters-in-law's cars	everybody's responsibility

8. Use the apostrophe to indicate the plural form of numbers, letters, and symbols.

He has three *i*'s in his name.
He gave me three 20's as change.

9. Use the apostrophe after the last of two or more nouns in order to indicate joint ownership.

Judy and Joan's locker	Joe and Al's car

10. Use the apostrophe after each noun in order to indicate individual ownership.

    Judy's and Joan's lockers   Joe's and Al's cars

11. The apostrophe is generally omitted in names of organizations, magazines, etc., by the organization or magazine itself.

    State Teachers College   Bankers Trust Company

ASTERISKS

The asterisk (*) is used infrequently.

1. Use the asterisk to refer the reader to a footnote at the bottom of the page.

> "It's been noted of Vermont winters that when one isn't currently in progress, one either will be shortly or was recently."*

2. Use the asterisk to indicate the omission of words that are unfit for printing or the omission of an entire paragraph.

> How dare you call him a ***!

> It is of no consequence to Sir Thomas whether or not her visit proves enjoyable so long as she learns to respect the wealth that she has lived in at Mansfield.

>   *   *   *

> Jane's stay at Portsmouth does, in fact, make her long for her childhood home, though not for the reasons Sir Thomas had intended.

DIAGONALS (OR SLASHES)

1. Use the diagonal or slash (/) in certain abbreviations and expressions of time.

    c/o (care of)   3/4 (fraction)
    B/L (bill of lading)   1987/88

2. Use the diagonal for *and/or* expressions.

    Sales/advertising will be located in this office.

---

*Brian Vachon, "Winter in Vermont," *Vista*, Winter 1981–82, p. 4.

CHAPTER THIRTEEN

COMMONLY CONFUSED WORDS

COMMONLY CONFUSED WORDS

accept (v)	to take
except (prep)	other than
access (n)	right to enter, admittance
assess (v)	to set a value
excess (n/adj)	extra
ad (n)	short for *advertisement*
add (v)	to increase
adapt (v)	to adjust
adept (adj)	skilled
adopt (v)	take as your own
addition (n)	something added
edition (n)	published work
adverse (adj)	hostile
averse (adj)	unwilling
advice (n)	recommendation
advise (v)	to give an opinion
affect (v)	to influence
effect (n/v)	result/to bring about
already (adv/adj)	previously
all ready (adj)	all prepared
alright	nonstandard English for *all right*
all right	entirely correct
altar (n)	part of church
alter (v)	to change *(notice the **a-e** correlation)*
altogether (adv)	entirely
all together (adv)	everyone in one group

among (prep)	three or more (*Among the three of them*)
between (prep)	two (*Between the two of them*)
amount (n)	refers to things in bulk or mass
number (n)	refers to countable items and people
appraise (v)	to estimate
apprise (v)	to notify
assistance (n)	help
assistants (n)	those who help
bare (n)	naked, no more than
bear (v)	to carry
beside (prep)	alongside
besides (prep)	in addition to
biannual (adj)	twice a year
biennial (adj)	every two years
brake (n/v)	device for stopping motion/ · to stop using a brake
break (n/v)	fracture/to breach
canvas (n)	coarse cloth
canvass (v)	to solicit
capital (n/adj)	official city of a state, money/ serious, chief
capitol (n)	building which houses state lesiglature
Capitol (n)	building in Washington, DC
cheap (adj)	inferior
inexpensive (adj)	low in cost
choose (v)	to select
chose (v)	past tense of *choose*
cite (v)	to summon
sight (n)	that which is seen
site (n)	location
coarse (adj)	rough
course (n)	direction, series of studies
complement (n/v)	that which comp**le**tes/ to comp**le**te (*Notice the **le** correlation*)
compliment (n/v)	expression of praise/to praise

correspondence (n)	letters
correspondents (n)	those who write letters
council (n)	assembly
counsel (n/v)	attorney/to advise
consul (n)	foreign representative
device (n)	mechanism
devise (v)	to plan
disburse (v)	to pay out
disperse (v)	to scatter
dual (adj)	double
duel (n)	formal fight
elicit (v)	to draw out
illicit (adj)	**ill**egal (*Notice the* **ill** *correlation*)
eminent (adj)	well-known
imminent	**imm**ediate (*Notice the* **imm** correlation)
ensure (v)	to make certain
insure (v)	to protect against
farther (adj)	greater distance
further (adv)	to a greater degree
faze (v)	to embarrass
phase (n)	stage of development
fewer (adj)	modifies plural nouns
less (adj)	modifies singular nouns
formally (adv)	in a **formal** manner (*Notice the word* **formal**)
formerly (adv)	at a **former** time (*Notice the word* **former**)
forth (adv)	forward
fourth (n)	follows third (*Notice the number* **four**)
forward (adv)	ahead
foreword (n)	preface in a book (*Notice the word* **word**)
incite (v)	to stir to action
insight (n)	clear understanding
its (pron)	belonging to it
it's (contraction)	it is

knew (v)	past tense of *know*
new (adj)	not old
know (v)	to understand
no (adj)	not any
lay (v)	to place an object down
lie (v/n)	to recline/untruth
lead (n/v)	heavy metal/to guide
led (v)	past tense of *lead*
loose (v)	to set free
lose (v)	to suffer a loss, to mislay
loss (n)	something lost
maybe (adv)	perhaps
may be (v)	might be
miner (n)	one who works in a mine
minor (n)	person under legal age
moral (n)	lesson relating to right and wrong
morale (n)	spirit
overdo (v)	to do in excess
overdue (adj)	past due
passed (v)	past tense of *pass*
past (n)	time gone by
patience (n)	endurance
patients (n)	persons receiving treatment
peace (n)	state of calm
piece (n)	portion
peer (n)	equal
pier (n)	wharf
persecute (v)	to oppress
prosecute (v)	to institute legal proceedings
personal (adj)	private
personnel (n)	staff
principal (n/adj)	sum of money, school official/ main, first in rank
principle (n)	rule *(Notice the **le** combination)*
respectfully (adv)	in a **respectful** manner *(Notice the word **respect**)*
respectively (adv)	in the order listed

right (adj/n)	correct/just privilege
rite (n)	formal ceremony
write (v)	to inscribe
role (n)	part in a play, function
roll (n)	register or list, small bread
should of	improper English
should have	proper English
stationary (adj)	fixed in place
stationery (n)	pap**er** *(Notice the **er** correlation)*
suit (n/v)	clothes/to please
suite (n)	set of rooms
sweet (adj)	having a sugary taste
than (conj)	comparison expressing exception
then (adv)	at that time, next
their (pron)	belonging to them
there (adv)	in that place
they're (contraction)	they are
therefor (adv)	for this, for it
therefore (adv)	consequently
to (prep)	toward
too (adv)	also
two (adj)	numeral
undo (v)	to open, to render ineffective
undue (adj)	improper, excessive
waive (v)	to forego
wave (n)	gesture, surge of water
weather (n/v)	condition/to come through safely
whether (conj)	if, in case
who's (contraction)	who is, who has
whose (pron)	possessive of *who*
your (pron)	belonging to you
you're (contraction)	you are

CHAPTER FOURTEEN

COMMONLY MISSPELLED WORDS

abbreviation
absence
absorption
accept
accessible
accommodate
accompanied
acknowledge
acquaintance
across
advantageous
affect
affiliated
a lot
already
ambiguity
among
analysis
anonymous
apparent
appearance
appreciate
appropriate
argument
arrangement
attendance
bankruptcy
beginning

believable
beneficial
benefited
bookkeeping
bulletin
business
calendar
campaign
cancel
cannot
category
cemetery
changeable
clientele
coming
committee
competition
concede
confident
conscientious
controversy
convenience
convenient
corroborate
criticism
defendant
depreciate
description

desirable
difference
disappoint
disbursement
discrepancy
dissatisfactory
dissipate
effect
eligible
embarrass
endeavor
endorsement
enthusiastic
environment
equipped
especially
exceed
excellent
except
exercise
exhaust
existence
experience
explanation
extension
extraordinary
familiar
feasible

February	oblige	receive
foreign	occasion	reciprocal
forty	occurred	recommend
fourth	occurrence	reference
government	omission	referred
grateful	omitted	referring
guarantee	opportunity	repetition
handwritten	opposite	requirement
height	original	restaurant
immediately	overdue	schedule
inasmuch as	paid	secretary
incidentally	pamphlet	separate
independence	parallel	sheriff
independent	paralyze	similar
indispensable	perseverance	sincerely
insistent	personal	stationary
interpret	personnel	stationery
its	persuade	strictly
jeopardize	photostat	subpoena
jewelry	physician	succeed
judgment	possession	successful
knowledge	practical	surprise
laboratory	practically	sympathy
leisure	precede	techniques
license	predictable	their
lien	preferred	there
likable	principal	too
litigation	principle	truly
loose	privilege	unanimous
lose	probably	undoubtedly
maintenance	procedure	unnecessary
mandatory	proceed	until
mediocre	professor	using
mileage	prosecute	vacuum
minimum	psychology	volume
miscellaneous	pursue	weather
misspelling	quantity	Wednesday
municipal	questionnaire	whether
necessary	really	withheld

CHAPTER FIFTEEN

FORMS OF ADDRESS

GOVERNMENT OFFICIALS

Person	Salutation	Closing
The President	Dear Mr./Mrs./Ms. President: Mr./Mrs./Ms. President:	Respectfully yours,
The Vice-President	Dear Mr./Mrs./Ms. Vice-President: Mr./Mrs./Ms. Vice-President:	Respectfully yours,
Chief Justice	Dear Mr./Madam Chief Justice: Sir/Madam:	Very truly yours Sincerely yours,
Cabinet Officers	Dear Mr./Madam Secretary: The Honorable . . . :	Very truly yours, Sincerely yours,
Senators	Dear Senator . . . : The Honorable . . . :	Very truly yours, Sincerely yours,
Representative	The Honorable . . . : Sir/Madam:	Very truly yours, Sincerely yours,
Governor	Dear Governor . . . : Sir/Madam:	Respectfully yours, Very sincerely yours,
State Senator	Dear Senator . . . : Sir/Madam:	Very truly yours, Sincerely yours,
State Representative	Dear Mr./Mrs./Ms. . . . . : Sir/Madam:	Very truly yours, Sincerely yours,
Mayor	Dear Mayor . . . : Dear Sir/Madam:	Very truly yours, Sincerely yours,
Ambassador	Dear Mr./Madam Ambassador: Sir/Madam:	Very truly yours, Sincerely yours,
Minister	Dear Mr./Madam Minister: Sir/Madam:	Very truly yours, Sincerely yours,

MILITARY PERSONNEL

Person	Salutation	Closing
General, USA*	Dear General . . . : Sir/Madam:	Very truly yours, Sincerely yours,
Lieutenant General	Dear General . . . : Sir/Madam:	Very truly yours, Sincerely yours,
Colonel	Dear Colonel:	Very truly yours, Sincerely yours,
Major	Dear Major . . . :	Very truly yours, Sincerely yours,
Captain	Dear Captain . . . :	Very truly yours, Sincerely yours,
Admiral, USN	Dear Admiral . . . :	Very truly yours, Sincerely yours,
Chaplain	Dear Chaplain . . . :	Very truly yours, Sincerely yours,

*United States Army.

RELIGIOUS OFFICIALS

Person	Salutation	Closing
Cardinal	Dear Cardinal . . . : Your Eminence:	Respectfully, Sincerely yours,
Archbishop	Dear Archbishop . . . : Your Excellency:	Respectfully, Sincerely yours,
Bishop	Dear Bishop . . . : Your Excellency:	Respectfully, Sincerely yours,
Monsignor	Dear Monsignor . . . : Right Reverend Monsignor:	Respectfully yours, Sincerely yours,
Priest	Reverend Father: Dear Father . . . :	Respectfully, Sincerely yours,
Mother Superior	Dear Reverend Mother: Dear Mother . . . :	Respectfully, Sincerely yours,
Nun	Dear Sister . . . : Dear Sister:	Respectfully, Sincerely yours,

Person	Salutation	Closing
Reverend	Reverend Sir:	Respectfully yours, Sincerely yours,
Rabbi	Dear Rabbi . . . : Sir:	Respectfully yours, Sincerely yours,

EDUCATION OFFICIALS

Person	Salutation	Closing
President	Dear Dr. . . . : Sir/Madam:	Very truly yours, Sincerely yours,
Dean	Dear Dean . . . : Dear Sir/Madam:	Very truly yours, Sincerely yours,
Professor	Dear Professor . . . : Dear Sir/Madam:	Very truly yours, Sincerely yours,
Instructor	Dear Mr. . . . : Dear Sir/Madam:	Very truly yours, Sincerely yours,

From The Desk of . . .

Sheryl Lindsell-Roberts

Following the birth of my two sons, Marc and Eric, I leaped out of the frying pan (in the kitchen) and into the fires of academia. Several years later—more than I'd like to remember—I received my Master's Degree in Business. In addition to writing books, I've been actively involved in education, marketing communications, and video productions. One video production was aired on cable television and was nominated for an award at the 1992 New England Video & Film Festival.

My other writings for Simon & Schuster, Inc., have included: *Office Professional's Quick Reference Handbook,* now in its Fourth Edition; *The Certified Professional Secretary; Data Entry for the Computer Operator; Proofreading and Editing for Word Processors;* and *Word Processing Mastery for Everyone.*

My husband and I live in Marlborough, Massachusetts, where we've recently built our dream house. When I'm not writing, I can be found illuminating the inner reaches of my spirit by traveling, photographing nature, skiing, or sailing *Worth th' Wait.*